ATVS Ē AGNOSCERENT SANCTĀ SINDONEM QVÆ QVOTĀNIS IV NON MAI CAMBERII
REVERENDISS FR LAMBERTI EP NICIEN PETRI LAMBERTI EP MAVRIANEN
R·F· ÆNEIS FORMIS EXPRIM CVRAVIT ROMÆ KL IANCIƆIƆ LXXIX

THE TRUE ICON

You have said, "Seek my face."
My heart says to you,
"Your face, Lord, do I seek."
Hide not your face from me.
Psalm 27: 8–9

Paul Badde

THE TRUE ICON

From the Shroud of Turin to the Veil of Manoppello

Translated by
Michael J. Miller

IGNATIUS PRESS   SAN FRANCISCO

Original German edition:
Das Grabtuch von Turin
© 2010 by Pattloch Verlag GmbH and Co. KG, Munich

Cover Images:

Front cover, top left: Negative of the face of Jesus on the first photo of the Shroud of Turin, taken May 28, 1898, by Secondo Pia

Front cover, bottom left: Image on the *sudarium* of Christ in Manoppello
Photograph by Paul Badde

Front cover, right: *The Holy Face of Christ*. Westphalen (ca. 1400).
From the gallery of paintings in the Kulturforum in Berlin
Photograph by Hildegard Schuhmann

Back cover, top: Pope Benedict XVI with Father Carmine Cucinelli in front of the image on the *sudarium* of Christ in Manoppello on September 1, 2006, on the first voluntary journey made by the Pope in Italy
Photograph by Paul Badde

Back cover, bottom: Pope Benedict XVI before the Holy Shroud in Turin, May 2, 2010
Photograph by *L'Osservatore Romano* Photo service

Cover design by John Herreid

© 2012 by Ignatius Press, San Francisco
All rights reserved
ISBN: 978-1-58617-591-7
Library of Congress Control Number 2011940709
Printed in Canada ∞

Dedicated to the memory of Domenico Petracca da Cese,
who died on September 17, 1978, as a pilgrim in Turin,
and for Brother Vincenzo D'Elpidio in Pescara

Why have you come to get in our way?
For you have come to get in our way,
and you yourself know it.
I do not know who you are,
and I do not want to know:
You may be He or you may be only His likeness…
Go now, and don't come back.
You must never, never come again!

—Fyodor M. Dostoyevsky
"The Grand Inquisitor" from *The Brothers Karamazov*

We desire to know God and we can know him through the face of Christ,
Benedict XVI keeps reminding us. Therefore we love the images that tradition
accredits as precious ways to glimpse this face, whether in Manoppello or in
Turin.

—Fr. Federico Lombardi, S.J.
Director of the Press Office of the Holy See
May 1, 2010

CONTENTS

THE SHROUD'S LONG PILGRIMAGE TO TURIN

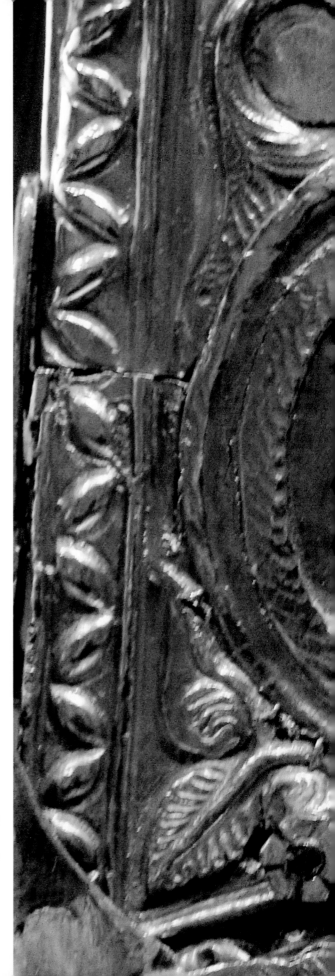

Medallion with the face of Christ on the oldest cross in Saint Peter's Basilica. Emperor Justin II sent it from Byzantium to Pope John III in Rome around the year 570.

Rantis in the Palestinian West Bank. The former Arimathea, the birthplace of Joseph, a member of the Sanhedrin, is not quite fifteen miles distant from Tel Aviv.

I had just been dreaming of Arimathea and had seen again in front of me the dusty village on the West Bank, when I opened my eyes. Outside, behind the window, the gentle hills of Tuscany glided past. Lying on my lap was *La Repubblica*, which I had bought at the train station in Turin. In an hour the express train would arrive in Rome. It was the final stage of a journey tracking down the Shroud of Turin that had just lasted eight days but had already taken decades to complete. "A medieval forgery. Here is proof!" a headline in the newspaper read, once again. Had I fallen asleep over it? The shroud a forgery? I had to laugh. I had experienced this many times before, but it was not always so funny.

It was a sort of cosmic déjà vu! I had already encountered many such debunking attempts, and very, very few of them have a purely scientific basis. For the old, bloodstained linen cloth, 4.36 by 1.10 meters [14.3 by 3.6 feet] in size, guards a scandalous, extremely provocative message. Somebody was once wrapped in this long sheet. It shows the shadow of the front and back side of a bearded man with severe wounds to his wrists, his feet, his head—actually everywhere. A man beaten to a pulp, the victim of torture! Immediately after his death another large wound must have been inflicted on him between two ribs. This "image" made out of blood and the cold sweat of death gives more precise information about

THE SHROUD'S LONG PILGRIMAGE TO TURIN

how a crucifixion was carried out than all the crucifixes in Europe's classrooms. It proves that in this cloth lay a man who underwent exactly the same thing as Jesus of Nazareth, who once was the great hope of many Jews shortly before the destruction of Jerusalem. No archaeological object is so consistent with every detail of the Passion narrative that was handed down to us about that Son of man in four ancient documents: described minutely, almost as though in fast motion, so exactly! No picture, no document anywhere on earth mirrors more precisely how Jesus met his death.

Initial photos from the year 1898, moreover, made the shroud famous for the fact that in its photographic negative the positive image of a face looks out at us. Naturally, that is puzzling. Nevertheless, any layman can see that the long linen cloth itself is neither a photo nor the film of a cosmic camera. If we take a cigar box and prick a tiny hole in the lid and fasten a piece of film inside to the bottom—thus constructing a primitive *camera obscura*—it would produce a more exact photo of any human being. Albrecht Dürer proved as early as 1516 that the cloth is not a painting either, when his attempt to produce a copy of it with brushstrokes failed. What we see has no contours, no drawing, no pigments—absolutely none whatsoever—and it rests only on the upper parts of the fibers. No one can say what it is exactly and how this image got onto the fabric. Nevertheless, a huge battle rages over the delicate, mysterious image. Some kneel down before it. Others are fiercely intent on debunking it as a forgery, over and over again.

Just as fanciful, therefore, is the history of debunkings that accompanies the shroud. Obviously such exposés try to prove above all that it was supposed to deceive the faithful. Once the BBC reported that a fourteenth-century French bishop had already found that it was "cunningly and deceitfully painted". He himself had never seen the shroud. The first likeness of the shroud is found in a manuscript from the year 1192 in Budapest. Nevertheless, it is supposed to date to around 1320, as scientists claim to have determined in 1988 by carbon dating techniques. Leonardo da Vinci too was "discovered" to have had a hand in producing the delicate image, and he was not born until 1452. The latest contributor to this series of discoveries was Luigi Garlaschelli from Pavia, a chemist (and self-taught specialist in astrology, as well as poltergeists and similar phenomena) who, at the behest and the expense of a group of Italian atheists and agnostics, had applied various sorts of paint to a student model, whose imprint on a sheet was supposed to serve this time as proof of the forgery of the Shroud of Turin. Yet genuine traces of blood (belonging to type AB+) can be found on the real shroud but not the slightest trace of pigments.

Does that surprise anyone? In the entire twentieth century, the shroud was exhibited only four times, in the years 1931, 1933, 1978 and 1998. After that, Pope John Paul II allowed it to be displayed publicly once more on the occasion of the Jubilee Year 2000. And then suddenly a new exhibition was announced for April 2010, to which millions of pilgrims would again hurry to Turin. Hardly anyone had figured on that date. Most people had thought it would be 2025. The year 2010 is not a Holy Year, as the years of such exhibitions often used to be called, nor is it a year like 1933, when Christendom celebrated the nineteen hundredth anniversary of Christ's death. The choice of date was simply due to the growing throng of pilgrims, especially from the East—their world, after all, had been cut off from the West for so long—who wanted to see the shroud once before they died, as Professor Giuseppe Ghiberti, the principal authorized agent of the Cardinal of Turin for the precious relic, told me.

Pope Benedict XVI had immediately agreed to the new exhibition and promised to take his place among the pilgrims. For the first time ever since it was thoroughly cleaned and restored in 2002 in a top-secret operation, the shroud would be displayed without any patches. And now reports like the one about the experiments by Professor Garlaschelli from Pavia started arriving and flying around before the event like swallows before the first barometric high of the summer. So now the fun was beginning again. All this fuss had amused me on many other occasions.

Indeed, many people who support the authenticity of the Shroud of Turin have—to put it mildly—hit on the strangest ways of convincing themselves and others that Jesus of Nazareth, after his execution around the year 30, was buried in Jerusalem in that very shroud. There is talk, for example, about a "nuclear flash" of the Resurrection, or about other sorts of cosmic evaporation that supposedly left traces on the long linen sheet. Dubious identifications [of the shroud] with various objects from the [Middle] East were extremely common for the early centuries [of the Christian era]. Barbara Frale, a paleographer from the secret Vatican archives, discovered beneath the face on the shroud a fragment of an Aramaic inscription, which experts have deciphered as "We have found." For the time being, everyone has to believe *Dottoressa* Frale, and I gladly believe her. One Monsieur Thierry Castex claims to have discovered the faint characters on the fabric as early as 1994 with a special optical procedure, but at that time he just could not yet interpret them. After the destruction of Jerusalem in the year A.D. 70 at the latest, Aramaic almost completely ceased

to play a role in Christian communities. The Letters of the Apostle Paul have been handed down only in [Koine] Greek. The inscription on the shroud must therefore date back to the first years of Christianity. Nice.

Years ago a French married couple, both researchers, investigated with the latest microdensitometer at the Institut d'Orsay several "shadows" on the shroud that they subsequently deciphered as the Greek inscription ΙΗΣΟΥ ΝΑΖΑΡΕ(Η)ΝΟΣ: *Jesou Nazarenos*. OK. I'm not really eager to verify their findings. "Do not try to prove what is more evident than any proof", the French writer Blaise Pascal once said. Yet it is also a question here of something other than proofs. Shortly before the start of my trip, my friend Bernhard called me. He said a lady had called him who had heard about my intention to look into the shroud again. Therefore, he should tell me the following information: three times the Greek Gospels explicitly mention the linen *sindon* that Joseph of Arimathea had bought for Jesus' burial.

That was not news to me. Years ago I traveled once from Jerusalem to Rantis for the express purpose of seeing whether there was still any memory there, behind the roadblocks, of that Sanhedrin member Joseph, who had ordered the purchase of the costly linen cloth in the Jerusalem bazaar for the burial of Jesus, whom the Romans had tortured to death as "King of the Jews" on Mount Golgotha outside the city gates. But ancient Arimathea today is just a godforsaken village on a flat hill

Photographic negative of the face of Jesus on the Shroud of Turin, as it was first recognized in 1898 when Secondo Pia produced the first [black-and-white] photograph of the relic.

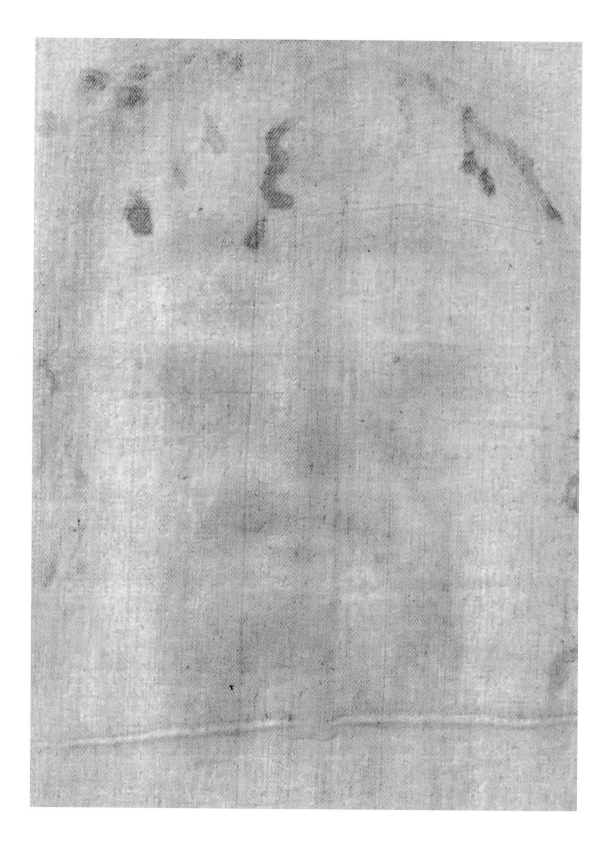

THE SHROUD'S LONG PILGRIMAGE TO TURIN

of the Palestinian West Bank, ten miles distant from Tel Aviv.

Yes, Bernhard said, chuckling, but now I should look at the three Scripture passages again anyway, add them up, divide by three and then see what Gospel passages I could find with the resulting combination. Then I should call him back. I took the Bible from the shelf and began to leaf through it. In Matthew it says, "Joseph took the body, and wrapped it in a clean linen shroud" (Mt 27:59). Mark writes in Mark 15:46, "And he [Joseph] bought a linen shroud, ... and laid him in a tomb which had been hewn out of the rock; and he rolled a stone against the door of the tomb." And in Luke 23:53 we read, "Then he took [Jesus' body] down and wrapped it in a linen shroud, and laid him in a rock-hewn tomb, where no one had ever yet been laid." It was not hard to add up the Scripture references and divide them by three: 27.59 + 15.46 + 23.53 = 66.58, divided by three = 22.193, or rounded to the nearest hundredth, 22.19. The Gospel of Mark has only sixteen chapters; the Gospel of John, twenty-one. So there was no passage to be found in them with this combination. In Matthew, though, the passage reads as follows: "And they brought him a coin. And Jesus said to them, 'Whose likeness and inscription is this?'" In Luke, in contrast, we read in chapter 22, verse 19: "And he took bread, and when he had given thanks he broke it and gave it to them, saying, 'This is my body which is given for you.'" I read it twice, three times: "Whose likeness is this?" "This is my body!" "Whose likeness is this?" "This is my body!"

Positive [color] photograph of the face that all pilgrims see when the relic is put on display during the rare exhibitions of the Santa Sindone in Turin.

Now I knew why Bernhard had chuckled before. For he knew as well as I did that it signifies nothing, proves nothing. The whole calculation is a coincidence. All the chapters and verses in the Gospels are late, arbitrary divisions, introduced so that theologians could more readily sling Bible verses at each other. Matthew, Mark, Luke and John, of course, wrote their Gospels without such subdivisions, even without periods and commas. Calculating the average and applying it back to the text is therefore a meaningless game. Yes, of course, and yet "This is my body!" as a hidden message of the Shroud of Turin—of course, that sounds mighty impressive. What author could fail to report the matter—even if it is of no use as proof.

That is why, with this anecdote, I would like to bid farewell to any and all proofs for or against the shroud. The investigations of the shroud have been so numerous that they cannot be repeated here. An international, interdisciplinary commission of researchers (STURP [Shroud of Turin Research Project]) has extracted exciting findings from the shroud in recent decades. The shroud has long been the most thoroughly investigated piece of fabric in the world. And after all that, the origin of the image that rests on its fibers remains *utterly inexplicable*. The decisive question, though, of whether it is the authentic burial cloth of Jesus cannot be answered with a fifty-fifty compromise. After we weigh all the evidence, there is only a definite yes or no. If it is the burial cloth, then all conclusive arguments add nothing to it. If it is not, then all the proofs for or against it can do nothing to change that. Basically, therefore, in answering the question, one is dealing with a personal decision, as with every genuine question of faith. This decision can be made only in freedom. "Both the believer and the unbeliever meet in doubt", share, each in his own way, doubt and belief if they do not hide from themselves and from the truth (*Introduction to Christianity* [San Francisco: Ignatius Press, 2004], pp. 46–47) Joseph Ratzinger once wrote. Maybe. Their paths separate there too, though—and also in faith.

the question: *What if it is?* The shroud, then, in this book, will not be defended against the arguments of its many opponents but rather will serve as a foil for a completely different experiment. For Christ's tomb is described by John in only twelve verses. He does not say

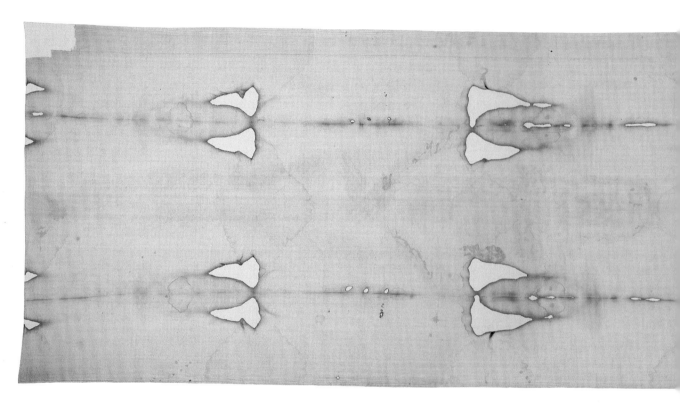

For even in the Catholic Church, my position is not an article of faith. I doubt—frankly—a lot of things. I doubt the latest news, I doubt my telephone bills and many prescriptions, and so on, but not that the Shroud of Turin accommodated Jesus of Nazareth after his death for two nights and a Sabbath. That is a position that the overwhelming majority of humanity *does not share.*

In the pages that follow, therefore, I intend to pursue a reverse inquiry. Not the question of whether the shroud is genuine but rather

that it was empty. Instead, in that brief passage he spends four verses writing about the cloths that he found there. Opponents of the shroud therefore say that it was fabricated so as to correspond to the text. It was a forgery to substantiate a lie. I say, on the other hand: This cloth is the relic of a true statement. Against all probability it has survived. There was talk about cloths already in the first documents of Christian history—and now here we have a cloth that corresponds perfectly to that talk. All the Gospels speak about this cloth. What

THE SHROUD'S LONG PILGRIMAGE TO TURIN

a weight of converging evidence! Not one contradictory indication separates it from the hypothesis that we truly have that cloth before our eyes in Turin. If we were in a court of law, the shroud would easily win any circumstantial case. It would be confirmed officially that contributed by various landscapes where the shroud must have been located.

In the West the whereabouts of the shroud have been meticulously documented since the year 1356 at least—whether in Lirey, Saint-Hippolyte, Vercelli, Chambéry or Turin. But if

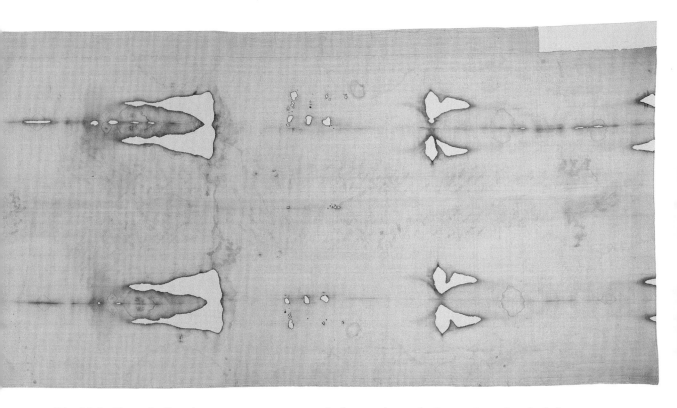

The Holy Shroud after the 2002 restoration with the scorch marks from 1531. On the left is seen the front side of the Crucified; on the right, the back side.

it is identical with the "clean linen" cloth that Joseph of Arimathea bought for Jesus. In our time Dr. Markus van den Hövel of Bochum, a judge, has taken the trouble to go through the process of evaluating the evidence again. And his judgment is unambiguous. Forensics has been busy too. In the 1970s Dr. Max Frei of Zürich discovered on the cloth by a special procedure a wide variety of plant pollens we follow the trail of the pollen hidden in this fabric, then the shroud must also have been in Jerusalem, the region between the Euphrates and Tigris Rivers, and in Constantinople. We will investigate all these places: from Jerusalem to Turin, via Constantinople, Paris, Lirey, Chambéry and Pinerolo. It is an itinerary that no navigation system can chart. It is too old and does not follow the course of modern roads. The way of the shroud leads through vast deserts, ancient cities and profound silence. Vercelli in the rice fields of the Po Valley is part of it, along with Montevergine in the south, to which the shroud was brought to safeguard it from the German Wehrmacht. The route leads past waterfalls and over dizzying, narrow mountain passes, where it is better not to run into anyone. It leads over high plateaus, where all paths disappear at the horizon; through deep, deep woods; through forgotten valleys and vaporous, drifting clouds to the narrow, serpentine paths on Mont Cenis along which the shroud was at last brought in solemn procession to Turin. Before setting out on this journey, let us first look again at the map of sufferings that is etched onto the shroud.

"The Shroud is an icon written in blood. Every trace of blood speaks of love and of life." —Pope Benedict XVI in his meditation in front of the Holy Shroud in Turin, May 2, 2010

THE MAP
OF HIS
SUFFERINGS

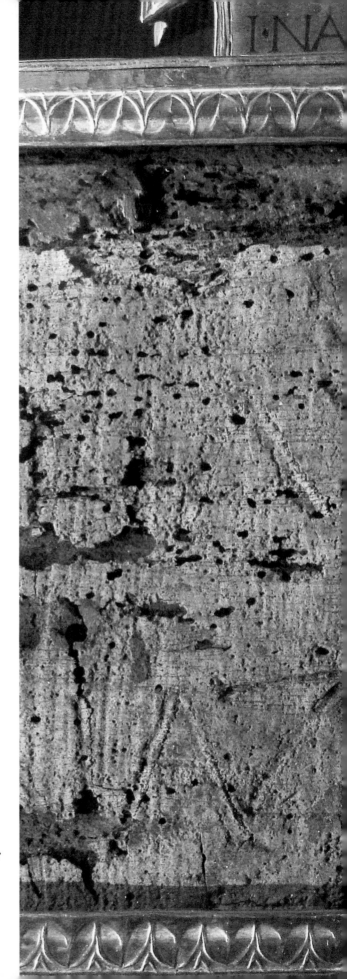

The Titulus Crucis, the panel in the Basilica Santa Croce in Gerusalemme in Rome with the inscription "Jesus of Nazareth, King of the Jews" in Hebrew, Greek and Latin.

Someone who knows what he is looking for and is otherwise acquainted with it only from photos or books is most surprised on his first encounter with the mysterious cloth by the peaceful expression on Jesus' face. No one knows, as we said, how and by what means this shadowy portrait appeared and why it has not faded away by now. This much is clear: Jesus was severely tortured before he was laid on the right half of this four-meter-long expanse of cloth and covered with the left half. The left cheek is swollen. On his back more than a hundred lashes can be counted. The shroud is strewn with the traces of the blows that had rained down on him. His head had lain in the middle; the sheet covered his bloody feet. A gracious hand crossed his slender hands in death over his private parts—where the star-shaped course of the bloodstains around a ghastly wound in his left wrist still reveals that he must have strained again and again on the cross so as to be able to draw his last breath. Along the forehead and from the back of the head, blood oozes from the hair. The flies—around the eyes, on the streaming blood and in the wounds—may have been the worst of all. Or did he not even feel them anymore amid all the other torments? One bloodstain on his right side is so large that one could easily have placed three fingers into the open wound that the shroud once covered at that spot. Blood and serum ran out of that wound and down his back as he lay: cadaveric blood, the "blood of the soul", as it was called in antiquity.

This is the fist-sized wound into which doubting Thomas placed his hand—Thomas, the patron saint of the incredulous. Jesus was already dead when this wound was inflicted on him. All the other wounds were blows to his living body, his back, chest, arms and legs. The right cheek has swollen up to the eye, the eyebrows too; parts of the matted beard have been torn out; the shoulders have been horribly mistreated. The back and all four limbs are littered with stripes from the scourges. Only above the left foot is there a half a hand's breadth without wounds. He was streaming with blood all over. It is as though he sweated blood, on his back, on his buttocks, his arms and legs, above, below, front and back. But is the whole thing a picture?

The problem already starts there. It is an original image, no doubt, but it lacks almost everything that makes an image an image: on the large cloth, as already noted, we find not a single line and not a bit of pigment—except for the many bloodstains. Yet they are just not part of the shadowy image. Even a blind man with a cane can see that it is not a painting. The bloodstains on the linen cloth, the water stains and the scorch marks are visible and can be explained, but there is still no explanation for the origin of this human shadow. It is the earliest photograph in history, some say. But that too, of course, is nonsense. My photos look different, as do the photos of those who maintain that the shroud is a "photo"—no question about it. In the first place it is a long panel of grayish-beige material with a complicated weave in a herringbone pattern, which one could take for a long tablecloth. It is the largest extant piece of textile that has come down to us from antiquity. No single object has been more precisely and intensively examined in the past century.

Having noted that, we can say the following. First, there are three "images" superimposed on each other on the long panel of cloth, two of them visible—one of them negative and the other positive—and one invisible. The first is completely colorless, entirely without contours, consisting solely of the interior coloring of the fibers, so delicate that you scarcely perceive it, and unique. In the picture gallery of

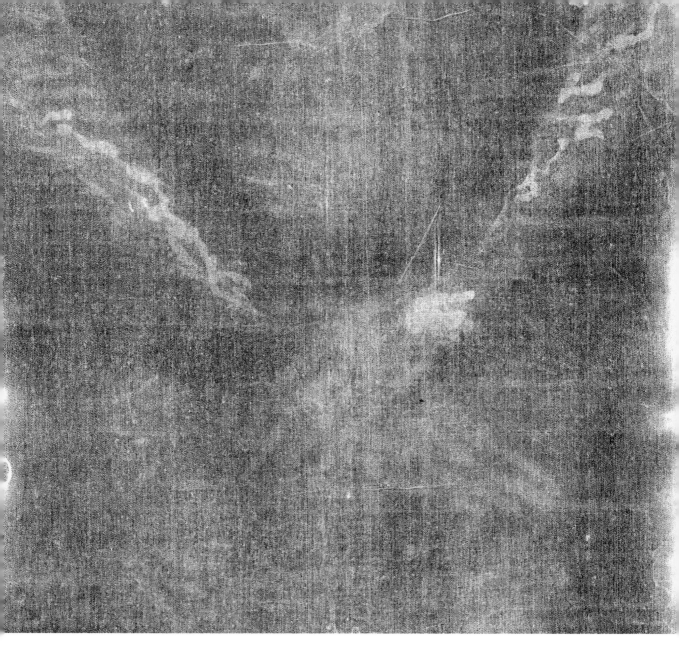

Detail of the shroud (shown in negative) with the hands folded over the private parts. The blood (shown in white) flows upward here because on the cross it ran down the arms.

the past two millennia there is nothing comparable to "Image 1", except possibly the shadow of the victims of Hiroshima that the atom bomb branded onto many exterior walls and interior partitions in Hiroshima in 1945. But even this comparison is immediately misleading. For those silhouettes have neither nose nor mouth. When it is completely unrolled, the shroud depicts a tortured man, about 1.8 meters [5 feet, 11 inches] tall, lying down, with a front and rear view, as though he had been placed on one end of the shroud and then covered with the other end. That is the delicate negative, which has already misled so many to consider the image some kind of cosmic photograph, ever since Secondo Pia, an amateur photographer from Asti, took the first photo of the shroud in Turin on May 28, 1898, and thereby discovered that on the negative of a photographic plate this double image of Jesus on the cloth first appears to us in the manner in which we normally look at the world. It is a paradox difficult to explain: the negative of this image is positive! Only the artificial reversal of its degrees of brightness made it possible to see then for the first time the world-famous portrait on the shroud that every child knows today.

"Image 2" is much more robust. It is the only real "painting" on this odd sheet, one that was not "painted" with a brush, of course, but with blood and serum flowing from wounds on the legs, the feet, the back, the arms, and the head; it also includes scorch marks and watermarks [from a nearby fire that was doused], and charred edges and patches. That is the positive image. Together the two images show Jesus as a scourged, crucified man. But to say that it shows a crucified man tells only the half of it. Rather, it was only through this shroud that we learned specifically what a crucifixion is. The nails were driven through his wrists and feet, not through his palms. That was done so that the weight of the body would not tear through the flesh. As a result, the thumbs were cramped inward toward the palms by the injury to the *nervus medianus*. Blood flowed

down the arms from the hands. He had a black eye. Only a few hours earlier he must have sustained a brutal blow to the face, much more than a slap. The upper part of the nose too is swollen. The sole of the right foot imprinted blood on the sheet as though with a stamp. Blood streams from the hair in the front and back from the cap made of thorn branches that the executioners had previously beaten onto his head as a crown.

Nothing about "Image 2" shocked me so much, however, as the fact that it shows Jesus naked. He is lying there as the Roman legionaries had nailed him to the stake, as naked as on the day when his Mother gave birth to him. Not a single thread covered the back of his body either. So the blood ran completely unobstructed down the stark-naked body to the legs. Obviously, I am not the only person to find that disturbing. On almost all paintings and frescoes that depict [the image on] the linen sheet, a cloth was wrapped around Jesus' hips for modesty's sake. No copy is as radically realistic as the original.

"Image 3", finally, is a text that for centuries was completely illegible; only in recent decades have investigators begun to decipher it. Besides the blood of Jesus, more bits of information adhere to this completely and utterly unique scroll than we can count stars in the sky. From the wealth of data that this pictorial text has already yielded since, the following observations by and large are considered today to be undisputed findings: The

A nail from Christ's crucifixion with a Byzantine sheath from the treasury of the cathedral in Trier (left) and the pillar of the scourging behind the Church of the Agony in Jerusalem (right).

The Map of His Sufferings

weave points to ancient origins in the Near East, since it was known in the West only from the beginning of the modern era. The blood that was not washed away from the feverishly hot corpse corresponds to the ancient Jewish tradition of burial, according to which blood was essentially the "seat of human life" and was buried along with the body in several cloths. Likewise, traces of aloe and myrrh have been found in the shroud, traces of a phylactery (a headband containing a written prayer and worn around the forehead), and the impression of a Roman bronze coin depicting an augur's staff, of the sort that the procurator Pontius Pilate had struck in the year A.D. 29/30 in Jerusalem. On the imprint of Jesus'

right heel, aragonite was found, and also on the knee. Aragonite is a rare sort of limestone that was brought to light many times in the excavations of the bazaar in Jerusalem. It was the dirt on the streets. The shroud therefore not only gives a new account of the Passion narrative in the Gospels but also completes it with other events that were handed down only by popular piety and in an oral tradition—such as, in this case, the repeated falls of Jesus on his way of the cross to Calvary. First of all, then, the map of sufferings on the shroud leads us too back to the streets and alleys of Jerusalem, on the eve of the Jewish feast of Passover, as the great curtain in the Temple was torn from top to bottom.

Splinter of the Holy Cross in a reliquary from the treasury in the cathedral of Trier (left) and the uncovered peak of Golgotha (Mount Calvary) in the Church of the Holy Sepulcher in Jerusalem.

EARTHQUAKE IN JERUSALEM

View of the old city of Jerusalem with the gold cupola of the Muslim Dome of the Rock at the site of the former Temple of the Jews. Behind it, the Mount of Olives.

Pascha, *Pessach*: the feast of the Passover of the Lord. From our house to the sacred tomb of Christ in the Church of the Holy Sepulcher was a distance of just under three hundred meters [less than a quarter mile]. On foot, through the angular old city and the bazaar, it took about fifteen minutes. In winter it was still dark; in the summer the sun already was climbing over the Mount of Olives into the eastern sky as I rushed down the great steps of the stairway to the Gate of Damascus, so as to hurry early in the morning through the labyrinth of the bazaar and the tunnel of Olive Street to the little room where Jesus of Nazareth, on the evening of April 6 in the year 30, was wrapped in linens "as is the burial custom of the Jews" [Jn 19:40] and was buried, after the lance of a Roman legionary had pierced him and verified the death of the Crucified.

The chamber is a magnet for all Christendom, yet in the days of the most recent intifada, as the streams of pilgrims were reduced to a trickle, it often belonged to me almost exclusively. I could still draw it blindfolded now: the low entrance; the little, narrow room beyond it; the small corridor to the left; and on the right, beside it, the stone bench on which the body was reposed. There he lay, wrapped in cloths as though in a cocoon. This is where it all took place. Joseph, the member of the Sanhedrin, or high council, had already had this room carved out of the rock for himself as his tomb. But then he had given it to the dead Jesus, who had fallen victim to the death sentence of that same council. Here Jesus lay in the long, precious linen cloth that Joseph had bought for him on the eve of the Paschal feast. Several days earlier Mary of Bethany had broken a vial of spikenard, which had cost a small fortune, and anointed him with the contents. Jesus was killed like a criminal. He was buried like a king.

And now it was Passover again. It was already dark. The streets of Jerusalem had grown quiet. An extremely learned, elegantly dressed older gentleman from Europe had visited us, a researcher with a Protestant background, who had studied the Shroud of Turin more intensively than any other person whom I had met in my life until then. I knew him from Turin; now he came to visit us on Helena Hamalka Street for dinner. Bread and olive oil were still on the table; we poured some more wine and told about our investigations in the Holy Land, while he told stories from his life as a researcher and reported a series of new findings about the shroud in recent years. He had just made some new discoveries, again, about the woven structure of ancient textiles in the Holy Land, which corresponded to the linen cloth of Turin. What he found especially remarkable, however, was something else that he had experienced not long before. At another dinner, another scholar had rather naively asked him the most crucial question about the shroud: whether he *really believed* that it is authentic and comes from Christ's tomb. "Yes", he answered. Nothing more. But he gave this reply for the first time in his long life as a researcher. At that same moment, the crystal of the wineglass in front of him suddenly shattered into a thousand pieces. "Without any external influence, you see? It just happened. I was terribly frightened. But you must not tell anyone else about it!" he immediately added, quite agitated, and I saw in the dim light of the lamp how he blushed.

That is why I do not want to tell anyone else about it either. Once again: What does it prove? Timidity? Human respect and fear of the frowns, the raised eyebrows of many colleagues at the university? Worry about not being taken seriously anymore as a scientist? Oh well. Stories of this sort flutter around

Dawn over the city wall of Jerusalem. In the distance—about 70 kilometers [43 miles] away— the silhouette of the mountains of Moab, in modern Jordan.

the tomb of the incredible Resurrection of Christ from the dead like butterflies on a spring meadow. Sure, because after all, the empty tomb is "the very heart of the Church", as Pope Benedict XVI said here on Friday, May 15, 2009. He too was therefore "cut to the heart" by his encounter with this room. This occurred shortly before his departure from the Holy Land and flight back to Rome, and it was the moment when I too saw the Holy Sepulcher for the last time, wedged in with a group of journalists. The cathedral of the Crusaders was packed; it was so crowded that I could scarcely reach for my pen and notepad. Clouds of incense billowed at the height of the cupola over the Holy Sepulcher, in which the *Te Deum* sung by the Franciscans

still resounded. It was a climactic event in the Pope's pilgrimage through the Holy Land.

Previously he had spent several minutes kneeling in the Holy Sepulcher, as absorbed as a Carthusian, in silent, persevering prayer—at the place where the Lord "overcame the sting of death and opened the kingdom of heaven to all believers", as, quoting the Te Deum, the Pope said afterward. "Here Christ died and rose, never to die again. Here the history of humanity was decisively changed." After about twenty centuries, he, as the successor of Peter, now "following in the footsteps of the Apostle", returned to this Holy Sepulcher, so as to contemplate the mystery of the Resurrection here with his predecessor, Peter. Peter, indeed, was the very first to enter the chamber on Easter

The so-called Tomb of Absalom from the first century before Christ in the Kidron Valley, which Jesus passed by on his final walk in freedom.

morning, as John recorded in his evocative account. "Here Christ, the new Adam, taught us that evil never has the last word, that love is stronger than death, that our future, and the future of all humanity, lies in the hands of a faithful and provident God." God can "make all things new". History need not repeat itself. Memories can be healed. The bitterness of accusations and hostility can be overcome. Yes, this is the faith of the Christian world, which the pope focused into a few burning words as though under a magnifying glass. The old man was exhausted by the journey—and blissful.

Next he would climb Mount Calvary, and after that he would be driven back to the airport. But now, in front of that chamber that is the heart of the Christian world, he praised the "empty tomb" seven times in his short speech.

Strictly speaking, however, John did not talk about an *empty tomb* in his "evocative account" of Peter's visit to this place. "Then Simon Peter came, following him," the sole eyewitness writes instead at the decisive moment, "and went into the tomb; *he saw the linen cloths lying, and the napkin, which had been on his head*" [Jn 20:6–7]. Certainly one of those linen wrappings or cloths was the shroud that is revered today in Turin. *Othónia* is the word in the original Greek: cloths. The tomb was empty, then, inasmuch as nobody was there. It was not completely empty, however! Here once again we have the difference that makes the difference, as Gregory Bateson says. A seemingly incidental note, which might just as well have been omitted, suddenly moves into the center of attention and becomes the real key for everything (as with a perfect murder in which the culprit nevertheless left a trace of DNA on a fountain pen). Of course, it is quite understandable why the existence of the cloths faded from sight again immediately afterward. The Evangelist Luke mentions them with a single word, but Mark and Matthew do not mention them at all. Yet they were mentioned at a decisive place, and that is the decisive thing.

The Gospels concerning the Resurrection are written in a complex style that cuts from one scene to another—a technique that we are acquainted with from films. By no means are we dealing with a primitive, linear narrative from New Guinea, in which the village elder says, "And then this and then that and then something else", and so on. The Gospels show images—Cut!—and afterward other images—Cut!—and still other images; and like every good film, the Gospels tell a story also with the images that they do not show—a thoroughly coherent, extremely plausible and reasonable story. In this process of omission, the "cloths" survived. For they are essential to the event of that night.

There is another, similarly plausible, reason for the fact that for nearly two thousand years, we have looked right past the cloths in our haste, as though we had not seen them. Pious Jewish practice today and Jewish customs at the time of Jesus Christ may be different in many respects. In one point, however, there is a constant that has remained almost unchanged during the last two thousand years. That is the observance of the *standards of ritual cleanness*. This was a fixed code of commandments and prohibitions related to cooking, hygiene and all departments of life in general. The Book of Leviticus in the Bible, like a pomegranate full of seeds, contains hundreds of extremely precise instructions about what to do and what to avoid in order to lead a life pleasing to God. Likewise does the Mishnah, the book of oral traditions. These books help much to explain the riddle of how it was possible for Judaism to preserve itself, through all the dispersions and pogroms and the Holocaust, as a people set apart from all other peoples. The Hittites, the Canaanites and whatever else all the peoples of antiquity were called, did not manage to do that. And so one thing was absolutely the same among pious Jews then as it is today: various foods, objects and places were considered

Jerusalem's typical stone—which often seems to be held together by a network of veins—in the ruins of a Crusader church in the Jewish quarter.

Twilight over the Church of the Holy Sepulcher and the Resurrection of Christ. The domes arch over Mount Calvary and Christ's empty tomb.

taboo. "Kosher" is the ancient Jewish word for it. There is even a hierarchy of cleanness. A breaded pork chop covered with a cream sauce and garnished with shrimp, for example, is unclean through and through. Yet the most repulsive and most unclean things imaginable in this world are objects from a grave, objects that had come in contact with a corpse.

"What about it, dear Adam?" I therefore wrote in a recent e-mail to a Jewish friend in Jerusalem who had accepted baptism years ago. "Do the purity precepts still have any sort of secret force for you? Despite your baptism, do you still feel in any way bound to the subdivision of the world into *kosher* and *tref*—into clean and unclean parts?" Adam is a radical who wants to accomplish 200 percent whatever he sets out to do. This is the way he became a Christian too, which in Israel is

no trifling matter. At any rate, he deliberately broke with the Jewish laws. "I don't think so", he wrote back two days later. "I don't eat frogs—but snails and pork, sure. I avoid all contact, though, with anything having to do with the dead. Then I flinch instinctively and am afraid of uncleanness." Other than that, Adam fears neither death nor the devil. In this case, however, his reluctant soul apparently still preserves a thousand-year-old taboo, fixed as though in amber. After his Resurrection, Christ left his likeness on the shroud—a first-degree offense against the Jewish prohibition of images—but that was only one thing. The fact that this imaging took place on a burial cloth was the other, the utterly impossible, thing.

Burial cloths were absolutely taboo. Even touching something like that was out of the question! Honoring objects from a tomb was unthinkable. Christ's burial cloths too—especially—therefore could not be revered publicly but only in the private homes of the controversial followers of Jesus. It would have been the coup de grace, the ultimate argument against the "new way" that the apostles were following after Christ's Resurrection. Say what? Kneel down before a rag from a grave? Couldn't you just worship a pig at the same time? The golden calf at the foot of Mount Sinai was cleaner and more pleasing to God than that, even though the Israelites danced idolatrously around it while Moses was receiving the Ten Commandments on the mountain. The original Christian community could not have survived a week after the Resurrection with that reproach, especially in Jerusalem, in the heart of the Jewish world, where Jesus of Nazareth himself had hung on the cross the previous Friday. It simply would not do. After all, there was a mob in Jewish cities too, just as later there was a mob in the Christian cities along the Rhine River that stormed the Jewish synagogues when the Crusaders from that region set out for Jerusalem to free Christ's tomb from the hands of the Muslims. In short, it was not only prudent to hide Christ's burial cloths for the moment. It was a must.

This knowledge, which simply could not be publicized, must have been kept by the apostles under lock and key from the very start. Family secrets did not leave home. But this really was the home of the young Christian community, this hidden primordial document about the Passion and Resurrection of their Lord and Master. Can anyone, then, still be surprised by the "foul graves" of silence in which the shroud remained hidden during the first centuries?

Nevertheless, are there not references to the shroud from the early, apostolic period? Yes, perhaps. In chapter 10 of the Acts of the Apostles, for instance, the Evangelist Luke tells about a remarkable vision of the apostle Peter in the port city of Joppa (today Jaffa near Tel Aviv).

> Peter went up on the housetop to pray, about the sixth hour. And he became hungry and desired something to eat; but while they were preparing it, he fell into a trance and saw the heaven opened, and something descending, *like a great sheet*, let down by four corners upon the earth. In it were all kinds of animals and reptiles and birds of the air. And there came a voice to him, "Rise, Peter; kill and eat." But Peter said, "No, Lord; for I

Dream and reality in East Jerusalem. The dream: a rusty bicycle. The reality: a hungry donkey in a stall.

have never eaten anything that is common or unclean." And the voice came to him again a second time, "What God has cleansed, you must not call common." This happened three times, and the thing was taken up at once to heaven.

Now … Peter was inwardly perplexed as to what the vision which he had seen might mean. [Acts 10:9–17; italics added]

Doesn't the "great sheet" in this vision sound suspiciously like the other long sheet of uncleanness that was already being preserved then in the original Christian community—precisely because of the unclean foods that are served on it? Was that what was going through Peter's head as he looked for the meaning of it? Was it a coded message about the hidden shroud of Christ? Yes, it could be. But that is naturally pure speculation; there is no longer any way of proving it. No one can doubt, on the other hand, what Jesus said again and again during his lifetime about the old Jewish concept of cleanness and uncleanness, as the Evangelist Mark, for instance, relates when he writes in chapter 7:

And [Jesus] called the people to him again, and said to them, "Hear me, all of you, and understand: there is nothing outside a man which by going into him can defile him; but the things which come out of a man are what defile him." And when he had entered the house, and left the people, his disciples asked him about the parable. And he said to them, "Then are you also without understanding? Do you not see that whatever goes into a man from outside cannot defile him, since it enters, not his heart but his stomach, and so passes on?" (Thus he declared all foods clean.) And he said, "What comes out of a man is what defiles a man. For from within, out of the heart of man, come evil thoughts, fornication, theft, murder, adultery, coveting,

wickedness, deceit, licentiousness, envy, slander, pride, foolishness. All these evil things come from within, and they defile a man." [Mk 7:14–23]

This was revolutionary. Ritual cleanness was an ever-recurrent point of contention in Jesus' debates with the Pharisees and the scribes. The conflict runs through all four Gospels. Again and again he was accused of having to do with the "unclean" members and the marginalized of Jewish society, with tax collectors, prostitutes and other sinners. With the cloths from the tomb, at any rate, the Jewish precept of cleanness fell into a perpetual darkness for the "new, worldwide Israel", as the early Church understood herself to be.

These cloths—more than anything else—must have brought about that tipping point in Jewish history; whatever notion we may have of it cannot be revolutionary enough. Like no other commandment, the radical distinction between clean and unclean stands also for the distinction between inside and outside, "one of us" and "one of them", "in" and "out", the good and the wicked, the (self-styled) just and the sinners, one people and another, one race and another. The purity precepts were (and are) the highest wall between Jews and Gentiles that had to be torn down so that the new Church of the apostles could arise, in the midst of which the existence of the burial cloths had broken the cleanness barrier for ever.

Since that time, nothing is unclean anymore to a Christian: no leper, no food, no urine, no scab, no infectious disease. For Christians since then, there are no more "no-go areas". That does not mean, of course, that this was not forgotten repeatedly also. Again and again the temptation arose to return in one way or another to the concept of cleanness. "Clean"

Khamsin over the square at the Gate of Damascus. The terrifying desert wind turns many spring days into night.

in Greek is *katharos*. The name of the medieval Cathars of southern France was derived from it. In Germany they were called *Ketzer*, heretics. They were the self-appointed "pure ones" who served already in the Middle Ages as precursors of later totalitarian systems. Europe's Christendom fought radically against them when it still had the strength to do so. Without this revolution at the beginning, however, a Mother Teresa in the slums of Calcutta would have been unthinkable, the way she bent over the dying to clean and wash them one last time. But back to Jesus of Nazareth. Isn't there almost a glimmering of his Father's humor in the fact that the "Holy One of Israel" left to his Jewish disciples after his death a precious treasure on extremely unclean fabric as the first relic?

After Christ's Resurrection, in any case, some twenty years passed until the last apostolic council in Jerusalem around the year 50, at which it was officially decided to abolish circumcision for newly baptized Christians and to dismiss the Jewish purity precepts from the teaching of the young Christian community. With the burial cloths, this decision was already anticipated on that first Easter night. With the burial cloths, one could suppose, the separation of the Christians from the Jews had also been carried out that night.

But that must be expressed more precisely. For after all, it was not a separation; it was a merger. It was the fusion of clean Jews and unclean Gentiles into a new people. It was the subversive assembly of those who shortly afterward in the great city of Antioch on the Orontes were called "Christians" for the first time, because they believed that Jesus was the "Christ", the "Messiah", the "Anointed One of God", in whom the [Son of the] Most High had become man and had shown his face. The Word of God, the Torah with its 248 commandments (and 365 prohibitions), had taken form and flesh in the 248 bones of his skeleton. John wrote that down too. From now on a believer had only to follow Jesus in order to go to heaven and attain eternal life. Henceforth it was no longer a question of cleanness and uncleanness. No other document in the early Christian world expresses that more clearly than the shroud. In it we hear, so to speak, how the old curtain in the old Temple tears from top to bottom, the curtain between the Holy and the unholy. Since then we know that we are all sinners and unclean but in a world that altogether is holy and loved by God.

I talked about all this until I was red in the face as we drove back from Turin to Rome. "But wait a minute", said Ellen behind the Genoa train station, just as we were driving out of one of the thousand tunnels into the bright light of the Ligurian sky. "You are talking the whole time about the old distinction between clean and unclean, between inside and outside, between us and them; you talk about 'in' and 'out', the good and the wicked, the just and the sinners, about one people and another, about one or the other race or class, and the wall between the Jews and Gentiles, et cetera. In discussing this tomb, though, shouldn't we be talking first and foremost about the distinction between life and death that was abolished

here? With the Resurrection of Jesus from the dead, didn't God altogether transform this unclean grave into a holy and clean tabernacle, into a new Ark of the Covenant where Christ, the incarnation of the Logos, had been preserved: the tormented body of his Son, the embodiment of the new law of love that is his from all eternity? The embodiment of love of enemies!"

I nearly choked. New medicine recently has thinned my blood a lot. But that wasn't the reason. It was that objection. For of course that was it: the primordial distinction that the burial cloths speak about first! I rubbed my eyes and sensed that the scales had fallen from them. What else does the tender majesty in the countenance on the Shroud of Turin show us but that a kindly face awaits us, too, beyond death—and, in this encounter, a judgment in which we realize our sins and judge ourselves by what we do and have done on earth? Here [on the shroud] God stands as a man before us, in the center of our faith. Here we see that we do not have to fear death. We should worry rather about a world and people who fear no judgment and no life after death—whether they are bankers or generals or our neighbors.

"But is there any indication in the Bible that these cloths were really preserved?" Ellen asked. Not directly. As for indirect evidence— that is a different matter. Around twenty pages after John's account of the Resurrection, we find the depiction of an astonishing episode from the early days of the Church. "And God did extraordinary miracles by the hands of Paul", we read in verse 11 of chapter 19 of the Acts of the Apostles. "Handkerchiefs or aprons were carried away from his body to the sick, and diseases left them and the evil spirits came out of them." After that, however, isn't the following compelling conclusion obvious?

View of Jerusalem from the pass on the Mount of Olives. To the west, the earth slopes from this vantage point to the Mediterranean Sea; to the east, to the Dead Sea.

If the cloths that were used incidentally by the Apostle Paul during his lifetime won such esteem in the early Christian community, then the cloths from the otherwise empty tomb that were so prominently mentioned by John would necessarily have been esteemed much more highly, would they not? They could not possibly have been disposed of as waste in a separate container, nor could they have been forgotten, left lying in the tomb, or thrown away. Weren't they, figuratively speaking, the first pages of the Good News about the Passion and Resurrection of Jesus Christ? But of course they were!

No doubt, therefore, the cloths must have been guarded from the very beginning by the Mother of Christ and the apostles as a precious treasure—even though not only their origin but their very existence absolutely had to be hidden immediately and concealed. For as we said, these first documents of the Gospel of Jesus Christ had been inscribed on the most unclean material that was imaginable in Judaism. So there was no other choice but to hide them immediately. Right away this makes several contradictions surrounding the news of the Resurrection much easier to understand, and also the fact that the cloths are scarcely mentioned at all by the other Evangelists. There were plausible and very good reasons for that.

But let us return again to the fact that only the eyewitness John expressly mentions the cloths that he himself and Peter found left

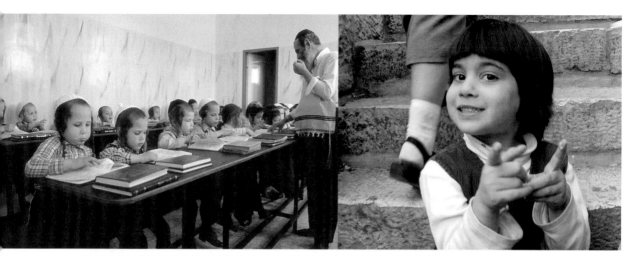

Orthodox Jewish children in Jerusalem. The purity precepts according to which they are raised have not changed in principle in over two thousand years.

behind in the tomb. Mark, in contrast, writes about how Mary Magdalene and two other women

> very early on the first day of the week… went to the tomb when the sun had risen. And they were saying to one another, "Who will roll away the stone for us from the door of the tomb?" And looking up, they saw that the stone was rolled back; for it was very large. And entering the tomb, they saw a young man sitting on the right side, dressed in a white robe; and they were amazed. And he said to them, "Do not be amazed; you seek Jesus of Nazareth, who was crucified. He has risen, he is not here; see the place where they laid him...." And they went out and fled from the tomb; for trembling and

astonishment had come upon them; and they said nothing to any one, for they were afraid. [Mk 16:2–8]

Matthew describes the discovery this way:

> Now after the sabbath, toward the dawn of the first day of the week, Mary Magdalene and the other Mary went to see the sepulchre. And behold, there was a great earthquake; for an angel of the Lord descended from heaven and came and rolled back the stone, and sat upon it. His appearance was like lightning, and his raiment white as snow. And for fear of him the guards trembled and became like dead men. But the angel said to the women, "Do not be afraid; for I know that you seek Jesus who was crucified. He is

EARTHQUAKE IN JERUSALEM

not here; for he has risen, as he said. Come, see the place where he lay." [Mt 28:1–6]

And Luke writes:

On the first day of the week, at early dawn, [the women] went to the tomb, taking the spices which they had prepared. And they found the stone rolled away from the tomb, but when they went in they did not find the body. While they were perplexed about this, behold, two men stood by them in dazzling apparel; and as they were frightened and bowed their faces to the ground, the men said to them, "Why do you seek the living among the dead? He is not here, but has risen. Remember how he told you, while he was still in Galilee, that the Son of man must be delivered into the hands of sinful men, and be crucified, and on the third day rise." And they remembered his words, and returning from the tomb they told all this to the eleven and to all the rest. Now it was Mary Magdalene and Joanna and Mary the mother of James and the other women with them who told this to the apostles; but these words seemed to them an idle tale, and they did not believe them. But Peter rose and ran to the tomb; stooping and looking in, *he saw the linen cloths by themselves*; and he went home wondering at what had happened. [Lk 24:1–12]

Are these contradictions? In Luke "the linen cloths" appear again fleetingly, with Peter "wondering" after he had seen them. Luke does not say that he came to believe as a result. Instead, he too writes about "two men … in dazzling apparel". Not Peter and John. These are angels, and angels are messengers from heaven. But a message from heaven was now inscribed on the linen cloths too. The bloody shroud had become clean, "dazzling apparel". The message was clear. No angel could have announced and revealed it more plainly. "He

is not here, but has risen. Come, see the place where he lay." All the burial cloths that John spoke about said the same thing. And the earthquake? Well now, Christ's Resurrection from the dead was in itself a seismic event of a sort that the earth had never experienced before. But the fact that these new glad tidings were written on the most unclean fabric possible shook the Jewish world to its foundations. The "great earthquake" in Matthew [28:2] was not just a metaphor or a sophisticated code. All the Evangelists had reason to speak and to write as they did about the earthquake and the messages and angels and cloths.

For taken together and read as a whole, they also make one last thing clear. I have already spoken about the modern, cinematic technique of the Gospels. That is to say, in cutting from one scene to another, certain images that are an integral part of this film are not actually shown. Accordingly, if you run the Gospel accounts by you again in slow motion, a significant detail stands out. It is the story about the guards at the tomb, who fell to the ground "like dead men" and afterward ran into the city to report to the high priest "all that had taken place" (Mt 28:11). So let us wind the film forward a bit once again. Then we see how Peter and John find the burial cloths in the empty tomb. John, who had arrived at the tomb first, stooped to look in, as he writes, and "saw the linen cloths lying there, but he did not go in. Then Simon Peter came, following him, and went into the tomb; he saw the linen cloths lying, and the napkin, which had been on his head, ... rolled up in a place by itself" [Jn 20:5–7].

After that, let us rewind to Matthew and watch the frightened women on their way from the tomb to the eleven apostles. Matthew goes on to write:

Southeastern battlement of the Jewish Temple plaza of King Herod from the time of Jesus, which since 632 has been a holy site of the Muslims.

While they were going, behold, some of the guard went into the city and told the chief priests all that had taken place. And when they had assembled with the elders and taken counsel, they gave a sum of money to the soldiers and said, "Tell people, 'His disciples came by night and stole him away while we were asleep.' And if this comes to the governor's ears, we will satisfy him and keep you out of trouble." So they took the money and did as they were directed; and this story has been spread among the Jews to this day. [Mt 28:11–15]

This episode, however, admits only one conclusion. First, the guards must have come to the tomb later than the apostles, and second, they must in fact have found it *completely empty*. When they arrived, the cloths were no longer lying there as John describes them. Before the arrival of the guards, Peter and John—in a sequence of our film that was not shot—must have taken the cloths with them. Quickly, in haste, immediately. Otherwise the accusation of the high priests and the claim of the guards would have been absurd. No one steals a corpse and removes the wrappings from it before carrying it away. Before they went to the high priests, the guards must have found the tomb already empty. If not, wouldn't the guards have taken possession of the cloths themselves and brought them along? Possibly. But where were the guards before that, in the dawn hour when first Mary Magdalene and then Peter and John came running to the tomb? We do not know. It is a rather chaotic scene that we are watching, like during an earthquake, really, when the ground gives way under your feet and everyone is concerned only about his own safety, and even the legendarily disciplined Roman legionaries "trembled" for fear and fell to the ground as though dead. In any case, before the daylight became bright and the guards had returned to the tomb, Peter and John must have quickly gathered up all the cloths and brought them to safety; otherwise this accusation could never have been leveled. Only a completely empty tomb could have justified a claim that the body had been stolen. Later on, this was also a decisive argument of the Church Fathers against these rumors and charges. No one could possibly speak credibly about the theft of the body if burial cloths had still been lying there. So it was, therefore.

And if it was not so? Because after all, despite the implied scenes in our film, we were not there and could not witness it ourselves! Then the following is true anyway: every infant, while still in its mother's womb, hears his mother's voice and, if he is lucky, his father's too. But as soon as he opens his eyes for the first time, he probably sees first the face of his mother rising very often over him, as round as a full moon. Not right at the beginning, yet very, very early on, therefore, visual perception assumes an important place in the life of every human being who is not born blind. So it is also with the faith of Christians. In the beginning was the Word. Yet very, very soon the image comes into view as well. Even in inanimate creation, the image was already there, before any eye could ever catch sight of it. By his Incarnation, God himself ultimately became image also in the merciful countenance of his Son—and in the Resurrection of Christ, he left behind an initial trace of that in the burial cloths, in the incorrupt face of Christ, which to this day death and decay have not been able to destroy.

FROM
THE EAST
TO
THE WEST

The abandoned tomb of the Apostle John in the ruins of Ephesus in Turkey. His Gospel contains the most precise eyewitness account of Christ's "empty tomb".

In contrast, one cannot say that the many places in which the shroud was kept on its long journey to us [in the West] have weathered the centuries intact. Turkey, for example, is riddled with the ruins of exquisite basilicas—a land of the Christian Apocalypse, with the silver sky of the Aegean Sea over it. The glimmering of sunlight in an oak grove. Wild alpine violets among the ruins. That is

Ephesus. A marble slab in a ruin, four turned freestanding columns at the four corners for a broken baldachin, a few lizards scurrying over the rubble. That is the tomb of John the Evangelist, about whom we spoke earlier. One can hardly imagine a greater contrast to the tomb of Peter in Rome, beneath the soaring lines of the largest dome in the world. Jesus loved John, to whom we owe the most impor-

Road through a pass in the French Alps before the Col du Mont Cenis, over which the shroud of Christ was brought from Chambéry to Pinerolo in March 1587.

tant account concerning the burial cloths and the brilliant formula that in Christ "the Word became flesh". John's tomb was empty, they say, when it was opened centuries ago. Only a handful of dust still lay on the floor, which the wind immediately carried off.

After Jesus' death, John had taken in Mary, the Mother of Jesus, whose house is still standing today opposite [the ruined church]

Hagia Sophia in Istanbul, formerly the principal church of the Byzantine Empire and an intermediate station for many relics on their way from East to West.

on Nightingale Hill. Before the end of her earthly life, however, he took her with him to Jerusalem, to the first and last apostolic Council of Jerusalem. Is it even thinkable that she did not have her Son's shroud in her baggage? "After Christ's Ascension, the Immaculate Virgin preserved an image that had developed on the Shroud", we read in a sixth-century Georgian document.

> She had received it from the hands of God himself and kept it with her at all times, so that she might always be able to contemplate the wondrously fair face of her Son.

Each time that she wanted to adore her Son, she stretched the image out to the east and prayed before it with her gaze on her Son and with open, uplifted hands. Before the burden of her life was finally taken from her, the apostles carried Mary on a stretcher into a cave. In this cave, they laid Mary down to die before the face of her Son.

And then? What happened to the shroud after Mary's death? Was it simply passed around from one apostle to another? Is it not logical to assume that this precious inheritance would have been dealt with just as we would

FROM THE EAST TO THE WEST

do today? Such a treasure stayed at first in the family. Now, always counted among Mary's relatives, since the days of the early Christian community, were a certain James, "the Lord's brother" [Gal 1:19] (who became the first bishop of Jerusalem), and Jude Thaddeus, from the inner circle of the apostles—two cousins of Jesus. Now, Jude Thaddeus is precisely the man who was mentioned more often than anyone else from that generation in connection with an image of Christ. There are a lot of richly embellished legends (and old icons and frescoes) that tell of how Jude Thaddeus brought an image of Christ to King Abgar V of Edessa. Today this city is Sanliurfa in East Anatolia (Turkey), located around 600 kilometers [370 miles] north of Jerusalem. At that time Aramaic was still spoken there; shortly afterward, in fact, the city became noted for its mysteriously early conversion to Christianity. In any case, the shroud initially was brought there safely and carefully hidden again—luckily for the shroud. And it would have good luck many other times on its long journey, most recently during the Second World War, when the motorized raiding parties of the German *Wehrmacht* advanced and it was secured in the Monastery of Montevergine beyond Avellino in Campagnia, and not, as planned, in the imposing Benedictine abbey on Monte Cassino, which was reputed to be one of the safest strongholds in Italy and by the end of the war was one heap of rubble.

There are libraries about the odyssey of the shroud. The most ink is spilled, however, on those parts of the story about which the least can be said with any certainty. There is agreement, however, that the shroud was rediscovered in the year 544 in Edessa, immured in the niche of a city gate (of which no stone has remained standing for ages). Reportedly the bishop, atop the city wall, showed it to the rejoicing populace. From then on, the shroud was known in the Byzantine world as the *mandylion*—purportedly from the Arabic word *mandel* (cloth)—or the "stamped image" (*ektypoma*), or "imprinted image" (*ekmageion*), and always in any case *acheiropoieton* also, which means "not made by human hands". Early on, it was also mysteriously called *tetradiplon* ("folded four times"). In the year 581 it is said to have been carried ahead of the Byzantine troops as a military standard in the battle of Constantinus against the Persians. In 622 the poet Pisides sang of the picture on the banner as the "image of the Logos: of the Word that formed the universe". Of course, in all these documents and legends from that period there is no mention of its provenance from Christ's tomb.

In the year 944 at the latest it probably arrived in Constantinople, the capital of the Eastern Roman Empire. The fascinating city

Typical mosaic of Christ on the upper level of Hagia Sophia with the noticeably swollen left cheek.

Figure of a demon on a cornice of the Cathedral of Notre Dame (above) and a stone crown of thorns around a tower of the Sainte Chapelle in Paris (right).

of Istanbul is today again the largest metropolis on the European mainland. On the upper level of Hagia Sophia we still find on the wall a magnificent mosaic of Christ, which we are not supposed to photograph. Yet the guard turns a blind eye to it. Isn't the Redeemer here modeled on the man from the shroud, with his part down the middle, the light beard, the swollen left cheek, and his majestic expression? Yet he has his eyes wide open. Other than that, no traces of the shroud can be found in Istanbul. We drink sweet tea and watch the cats in the streets. Byzantium, since its conquest by the Ottomans in the year 1453, has become a virtual realm, an empire of libraries, of obscure documents and treasures scattered about, of

Next spread: The monastery church of Lirey in Champagne, where Christ's burial cloth was exhibited in 1357 for the first time in Europe.

50

The Last Supper, above the main entrance to the Abbey Saint-Germain-de-Près in Paris with the decapitated Christ and his apostle.

museums and archives from all over the world, of seminars for specialists, in a bewildering labyrinth.

In this empire a certain Theophanes presented to the emperor Romanus on August 15, 944, a sacred relic, the *hagion mandylion*, which he had brought from Edessa to Constantinople. In the Biblioteca apostolica vaticana a Greek manuscript (in Codex vat. graec. 511) captures the event in the flowery oration of one Archdeacon Gregory. Based on the description in this speech, however, you probably could not issue a warrant for the arrest of the shroud. There was nothing to be seen on the cloth, said the king's sons, except a face. We encounter no further witnesses to the shroud's sojourn in Constantinople until the reign of Manuel I Comnenus (1148–1180). A

delegation from Hungary visited the emperor in 1150; we probably owe to one of its members the first graphic representation on which the *sindon* can be identified unambiguously, because for the first time it shows Jesus' dead body as on the shroud: totally naked, with the hands over the private parts and the thumbs cramped inward; this image is found in the Codex Pray from the year 1192, which today is preserved in the Budapest National Museum. The itinerary of the shroud then takes a decisive turn in the confusion of the sack of Constantinople by the Latin Crusaders on April 12–13, 1204. It was a catastrophe in which the *sindon* disappeared from the East— and all the circumstances of the theft are mysterious to this day, and afterward all traces of it disappear initially into obscurity.

In September 1241 a *toella sancta* was brought, along with other relics, to the court of King Louis IX of France—a "holy towel" that many researchers identify as the shroud. Two years before that, Louis had bought Christ's crown of thorns from King Baldwin II in Constantinople; by 1248 he had spent 40,000 pounds of gold to have the glass palace of the Sainte Chapelle constructed as a gleaming shrine for it. That horrendous price was nothing, though, compared to the 135,000 pounds that the crown of thorns itself had cost him. The golden reliquary in which the sacred instrument of torture was kept cost another 100,000 pounds. Jacobins melted it down in 1789. We walk our feet off in the churches of Paris trying to find some echo, some trace, however vague, of Christ's shroud, which of course could not be worth less than his crown of thorns. At the Sainte Chapelle even the filigree towers up above are wreathed with sharp stone crowns of thorns. There is nothing like it with regard to the shroud. While inside the glass cathedral, we search in vain with binoculars for the *sindon* on the gigantic windows. Countless stories from the Bible and the Crusades are recounted there in glowing pictures, but nothing about the linen cloth that Joseph of Arimathea had bought for the dead body of Jesus. At the front, in the choir, two angels—with their hands covered—reverently hold up the crown of thorns over the high altar to be venerated.

Inside Notre Dame we rest for a while in the dusk behind the high altar, where the crown of thorns is kept today in a dark, ruby-colored reliquary made of plastic. Little electric lights glimmer from inside the work of art; its contents were once considered in Europe to be worth half a kingdom. Instead of representations of the shroud, I photograph the gargoyles on the cornices of Notre Dame: they probably nest on every church roof—as well as in every heart—because those beasts know perfectly well where everything is at stake. The incendiaries of the French Revolution knew it too: back then they had a whore representing the goddess of Reason dance on the main altar in Notre Dame, and they struck the heads off statues of the saints wherever they found them. They were aiming at Christ in particular; they struck his head off whenever they could get hold of him. A God who showed his face was intolerable for those fanatics. I took a few more pictures of the portal of Saint-Germain, where over the entrance the beheaded Christ still sits at table at the Last Supper, and then we drove further to Lirey.

There, on the southern edge of Champagne, the shroud first appears in the history of the West. In 1353 it is said to have come into the possession of the knight Godefroid de Charny in Lirey. His wife, Jeanne de Vergy, was a direct descendant of Othon de la Roche, who was in Constantinmple 149 years before, when the imperial palace was plundered along with the Blachernae, the church in which the shroud had last been seen. You have to come to Lirey, however, to understand why something that no one had dared to exhibit previously in the Christian metropolises was suddenly put on public display. You would have to search for a long time to find a more abandoned spot than Lirey, in the midst of its loamy fields. Colorful apples galore lie this fall under the trees around the few half-timbered houses. Nothing suggests champagne. A sign on the door of the church in the middle of the secluded spot recommends asking Monsieur Jacques Chevrot (9, rue des Bas Clausais) for the keys. Does he also have books or documents about the *sindon* (which is still called the *soudarion* here)? No, nothing of the sort. "Just throw the keys in my mailbox afterward." More communicative than Monsieur Chevrot is the condition of the church. Sparrows flutter toward us as I open the portal. Dead flies and bird droppings cover the altar. Spider webs line an old cabinet, the door of which hangs askew on its hinges. A poem by François Villon is posted on the back wall of the church. Lirey no longer gleams. The shroud is better preserved than this church.

Precisely how and when the shroud arrived here is obscure. Godefroid de Charny was the royal standard-bearer and fell in battle on September 19, 1356, beside the king of France in the battle against the English at Poitiers. Only after that, in 1357, did his widow organize the first known exhibition of the shroud in front of the church in Lirey, which immediately attracted many pilgrims. The sources of our information about this are a commemorative medallion made of lead with the double image of Christ, which for the first time shows full-length the front and back sides on the sheet, and a vehement critique by the local bishop. The medallion, which was found in the mud of the Seine River, is the first unambiguous depiction of the shroud. Until then there had been many images of Christ, but never this double image. Today, at any rate, it seems that until that first exhibition the initial taboo had clung to the burial cloth like a long shadow of its extreme uncleanness in the world of Judaism where it had originated. Yet since the year 1357 every stage of its whereabouts in Europe is well documented.

Henri de Poitiers, the bishop of nearby Troyes, just could not believe that such a precious relic could have fallen into the hands of an insignificant widow, and he saw to it that the exhibition was terminated. For thirty-two years afterward the *sindon* disappeared again in the castle of the Charnys. But in 1389 it was exhibited again in Lirey, even more solemnly than before, "as though the very body of Christ our Lord were being laid out: by two priests vested in alb, stole and maniple, with the utmost reverence, burning torches, and on a platform constructed especially for that purpose". In these words Pierre d'Arcis, the new bishop of Troyes, severely criticized the event. In doing so he once again recalled the assessment of his predecessor, that it could only be a forgery.

"The facts of the matter are these, Holy Father", he went on to write to the pope.

> Some time ago in the Diocese of Troyes the dean of the monastery church of Lirey fraudulently and deceitfully, out of greed, not piety, merely for the sake of gain, obtained for his church a cunningly painted cloth on which the double image of a man, front and back, was craftily painted, whereby he fraudulently claims that this is the actual burial cloth in which our Redeemer Jesus Christ lay wrapped in the tomb and on which the complete image of the Savior with his wounds was imprinted. This tale has now been bruited about, not only in the kingdom of France but throughout the world, so that people came from everywhere to see it.

One reason why he thought that it must be a forgery was the fact that many theologians had declared that it could not be the true shroud of our Lord, since the Gospel reports nothing about such an image, and if it were true, it is completely implausible that it could have remained hidden until then. It was a shrewd argument. Yet the furious bishop had never seen the cloth personally. And this second exhibition had been organized by Godefroid II de Charny, the son of Jeanne de Vergy, who had obtained special permission to do so from Pope Clement VII. This pope was also the one who ended the debate at that time by generously allowing the exhibition of the shroud in

The monastery church of Saint-Hippolyte-sur-Doubs, where the shroud of Christ was kept from 1418 to 1452 and regularly exhibited on the banks of the Doubs River.

Lirey—provided, however, that it not be called the *sudarium* [Veronica's veil]. For that cloth was found in Rome, where it was shown regularly to pilgrims.

The controversy over the shroud was not about to end with that. In 1418 the canons regular of Lirey, for fear of marauding bands, entrusted it to Count de la Roche, the husband of Marguerite de Charny. It was goodbye forever and the beginning of a long legal dispute. The shroud remained in the Church of Saint-Hippolyte for thirty-four years, and neither the parliament in Dole nor the court of Besançon could induce the widow to give back the relic. Instead, in 1453 she conveyed it unlawfully yet in a legally binding way to the custody of the ducal house of Savoy, which in 1502 brought it to the chapel of their castle in Chambéry at the edge of the Alps. Louis I of Savoy conveyed to the widow, in exchange for the shroud, Verambon Castle near Geneva and other sources of income. It was the last change of owner until Umberto II of Savoy bequeathed the *Santa Sindone* to the *Santa Sede* (Holy See) 530 years later in his last will and testament, dated 1983. Therefore, its present owner is Benedict XVI. In a roundabout way, the shroud has returned now to the hands of the man whose predecessor had recovered it at the very beginning.

The countless byways and detours of this odyssey continue today, however, in the infinite halls of cyberspace, which have long since expanded the stuffy old libraries, and in the millions of blogs where anyone can say anything about everything and can disseminate speculations and claims unchecked. In this new world you can surf the Web in pursuit of your favorite theory about the shroud and arrive at any conclusion imaginable. There is no limit, either, to the possible outrageous errors. Day after day we had time to reflect on this, as we actually traced the *sindon* through the undulating hills of Champagne and the gorges of the Doubs, in the deep green of the Jura Mountains or past the glittering Lac de Bourget. Everywhere it was as if we were following the trail of a protective hand that again and again mysteriously rescued this cloth from a great number of dangers. In Saint-Hippolyte we viewed the meadow on the riverbank where the shroud had been exhibited outdoors at regular intervals. In the castle church of Chambéry we went behind the altar and inspected a stone niche resembling an empty eye socket, in which the chest with the shroud had been stored. This stone dungeon was the only thing that kept the shroud from burning on December 4, 1532, as the chapel in the Savoy palace went up in flames. Molten silver has nevertheless caused the fabric the greatest damage to date. Later on, the Jacobins would have been very happy to burn it up entirely, even though at that time the little city of the

Duke of Savoy was not yet part of France. So they just destroyed a memorial tablet over the main entrance that dedicated the chapel to the shroud of the Most Holy Redeemer. But by then the long sheet was in Turin: once again, half-illegally and cunningly, against the furious resistance of the populace of Chambéry, it had been carried off to safety in a final long procession. On its journey from the Orient to the Occident the *sindon* could have been incinerated, destroyed or lost a hundred times. Instances of plundering and theft and repeated breaches of the law saved it.

Niche behind the main altar of the palace chapel in Chambéry in the ancestral house of Savoy, where the shroud was kept from 1453 to 1578, with interruptions.

SUNKEN
GOLD

*Fresco in front of the motherhouse of
the Oblates of the Virgin Mary on the
Via Sommeiller in Pinerolo in the
Piedmont region commemorating the
arrival of the shroud of Christ in 1578.*

Pinerolo in the Piedmont region is located in the pine woods outside Turin, on the old pilgrimage route leading from France over the Alps to Rome, and it is surrounded by mountains on the north and west. It is a rust-colored beauty made up of crumbling brick walls, moss-covered steps and gravel streets, with doves on the wayside among pink blossoms at midday, and lined with French-style parks and boulevards that even in summer breathe the drowsiness of autumn. The cooking too is faintly reminiscent of French cuisine, as though centuries ago the treasures of Gaul had been carried down from the mountains through this little city into Italy.

So it was also on March 19, 1578, as Duchess Yolanda of Savoy, the widow of Amadeo IX and regent for her minor son Filiberto, arrived with her court after her arduous journey from the ancestral seat of the house of Savoy in Chambéry in the French Alps, over Mont Cenis, and through the Susa Valley to Pinerolo. She brought with her a great number of parcels that Jean Ranguis, prior of the Church of the Holy Sepulcher in Annecy, had entrusted to her, among them the extremely precious linen sheet that had been called *sindon Salvatoris nostri Jesu Christi* [the shroud of our Savior Jesus Christ] for the first time in Chambéry. With this title the long sheet was by now identified unquestioningly with the cloth described by the Evangelists Matthew, Mark and Luke in the first century as having been purchased by Joseph of Arimathea for Christ's burial. Now Charles Borromeo had hurried from Milan to welcome the precious relic. The most famous archbishop of his day was a great devotee of the face of Christ. Now he ardently awaited the opportunity to get to know also the large sheet with the image of the whole body.

The chest that was used to transport the shroud was adorned with crimson velvet. Silver locks protected its contents. Only a two days' journey separated the *Santa Sindone*, as it was now called in Italy, from the vault of the Basilica of Saint John at the royal palace of the house of Savoy in Turin, which was to be the final stop of the precious linen cloth on its pilgrimage. There it was to be solemnly exhibited again at last, as it had been before so often in France since the first display of the shroud in Lirey more than two hundred years previously. Yet archbishop Urbano Bonnivardi of Vercelli, to whom the duchess intended to entrust the education of her son, came to visit the duchess in Pinerolo and asked her, please, to allow the shroud to be shown to the people there too on Good Friday in public in front of the cathedral—like "Veronica's veil", which for 370 years had similarly been shown in Rome to the pilgrims during Holy Week from a balcony of the old Saint Peter's Basilica. So it happened.

It was the first public exhibition of the shroud in Italy, which nevertheless was soon forgotten once the spotlight was on the more splendid city of Turin. Only in the year 1898 did the scholar Cordero di Pamparato discover in the Savoyard archives a document listing the expenses that Prince Ludovico had incurred for the draped platform in front of the cathedral in Pinerolo in 1478. No other documentary evidence of this first exhibition of the *Santa Sindone* in Italy has been preserved.

The operative word here is "documentary", because this story was recounted over and over again in images, although with the passage of time they too attracted less and less notice. In the Piedmont region alone, many pictures record the final journey of the shroud of Christ over the Alps to Turin. However, this is especially true of Pinerolo. There we see in a lunette over the left main entrance to the cathedral a fresco that depicts the dead body of Jesus, hands crossed, being placed upon the

Street in Pinerolo through "French-style parks ... that even in summer breathe the drowsiness of autumn".

shroud in his Mother's lap, and over the right main entrance, two bishops, together with two angels, displaying the unfolded shroud.

On Musketeers Street also, not far from the cathedral, we find at one story above street level a peeling fresco on the exterior wall in which the Mother of God displays the shroud, perhaps with a saint and a Franciscan at her side (it is difficult to tell precisely). Right around the corner, however, on the Via Sommeiller, there is—again at the second-story level of an old *palazzo*—a depiction of the *sindon*, which may well be the only one of its kind in the whole world. Even I would never have found it and would certainly have missed it had not a pilgrim called my attention to it in an e-mail months before. "Can you tell me who that is depicted beside Mary?" I asked an elderly passerby as I stood below it in amazement. The

man stopped, looked up and shook his head. He lived four houses down but had never looked at it before. Therefore, we would have to interpret the picture ourselves.

It shows in a Baroque frame six people in a row holding a long sheet on which is imprinted, head to head, the back and front side of Jesus; again, unlike the original, a cloth is wrapped around his hips for modesty's sake. As for the individuals holding the cloth, Mary, the Mother of Jesus, stands in the middle. To the right of her [from the viewer's perspective] stand either Mary Magdalene or John the Evangelist, and Saint Francis; to the left, John the Baptist and Saint Dominic: and at the edge of the picture, Saint Joseph or Joseph of Arimathea. They can no longer be identified exactly. Did Charles Borromeo commission this fresco? If so, it must have been painted

Ciborium on a fresco in the grottoes under Saint Peter's Basilica in Rome; the inscription notes that the sudarium [Veronica's veil] had been kept in it since the year 708.

between 1578 and 1583. Completely clear, in any case, are three angels over the group that is holding the gigantic shroud with the indistinct figure of Christ: the little angel in the middle holds a little veil with an ocher-toned portrait of Christ with his eyes open.

The fresco on the Via Sommeiller adorns the motherhouse of the Congregation of the Oblates of the Virgin Mary. It is a grand old *palazzo*, in which only Father Alan from America keeps watch. The friendly priest is alone. He helps us in any way we ask and lets us photograph whatever we want from the second floor. "It would be a bigger miracle if the Shroud of Turin were *not* Christ's burial

cloth", he says with a smile as we leave. "In other words, if an artist in the Middle Ages had fabricated that cloth before the invention of photography and before people knew about many details of Christ's torture as it is described in the Gospels, that would be the *bigger miracle*." Other than that, unfortunately, he could not help us decipher the fresco on the wall of his house. In his files he found an article of a municipal archivist about the first exhibition.

Yet the picture itself speaks. For the little burial cloth above the large one can only be the holy *sudarium* (sweat cloth) from Rome, which in those days was displayed so regularly and so long and with such great solemnity in Rome. There is no doubt about that. In other words, it is the same cloth that Pope Benedict XVI went to see on September 1, 2006, in his first freely chosen trip within Italy by helicopter to a hill behind Manoppello and that he silently venerated in a tiny Capuchin church—the first pope to do so in four hundred years. This little town in the Abruzzi region is about 180 kilometers [112 miles] distant from Rome. How and when the *soudarion* [Veronica's veil] came to Rome is uncertain, and also how it disappeared again. This loss—or gain—may have occurred during the *sacco di Roma* in the year 1527, when the *soudarion* was safeguarded from the German *Landsknechte* [mercenaries] in much the same way as the shroud was later safeguarded from the raiding parties of the German Wehrmacht. Or maybe it was moved later. At any rate, it requires an explanation, and to do that I have to back up a bit here.

In the year 1578 this cloth had been copied so often by so many different painters that the police could have issued a very precise arrest warrant based on those paintings. The image shows the face of Christ on a transparent veil in delicate byssus colors, framed by shoulder-length hair parted in the middle and a sparse beard. The left cheek is slightly swollen, the mouth slightly open, and the eyes are open in an expression that is not included in the vocabulary of arrest warrants: perfectly merciful. Dante Alighieri refers to this face at a central point in his *Divine Comedy* (1307–1320). In the grottoes of Saint Peter's Basilica there are old frescoes that show a "ciborium" in which the cloth was allegedly kept in the Vatican since the year 708. But that could be an artificially early date. From 1208 on, however, Pope Innocent III had it carried in procession through the city each year. Since that time it was publicly known. Innocent even composed a special hymn for the delicate veil. During the first Holy Year, 1300, Boniface VIII ordered that the napkin be venerated regularly. It was the same cloth that prompted Clement VII to permit the exhibition of the large shroud in Lirey in 1392, provided that the cloth there would not be called *sudarium*, since that was in Rome in the custody of the pope. Here it is now again.

It is the *sudarium*, the *soudarion*, [the Greek term for] the "sweat cloth" of Christ, which John the Evangelist mentions in his account of Christ's Resurrection just as prominently as the *sindon*, or rather, even more prominently, without actually mentioning the image—for good reasons, as we will see later. In any case, it was not only the *sindon* that had survived without rotting away; the *soudarion* too, the "napkin, which had been on his head, not lying with the linen cloths but rolled up in a place by itself" [Jn 20:7], had withstood the ravages of time and was intact. Of course, that is incredible. Here in Pinerolo, though, we see them together for the first time. When the shroud came to Turin, the reputation of the *sudarium* came from Rome to meet it. Outside the gates of Turin this fresco combined once again what belonged together ever since John

told about these cloths in the same breath.

The original of the little cloth shown over the large one is only 17 by 24 centimeters [6.7 by 9.4 inches] and as fine as gossamer; someone standing in front of it cannot help but think afterward that it was this napkin and not the large shroud that the Byzantines carried into battle as a banner of victory on their campaigns against the armies of the Persians and the Muslims. This miraculous image of Christ is said to have been brought to King Abgar of Edessa by Jude Thaddeus. This image must also have been the one that the poet Georgios Pisides had in mind when in the seventh century he sang of the countenance on the military standard as an "image of the Logos". Once you have seen this veil, you can no longer imagine that the troops and fleets of the Eastern Roman Empire ever allowed the four-meter-long shroud to flutter in the wind ahead of them. The little cloth is wonderfully suited to clear up a great number of other contradictions, which scholarship in recent decades has needlessly labored to explain by means of reckless theories in its attempts to account for the itinerary of the Shroud of Turin through the first millennium.

For in the image on the *sudarium* in Manoppello, as we said, Christ has his eyes open, just as on countless portraits from the first millennium—and quite unlike the imprint of Christ on the linen cloth in Turin. This is very important. Here too—as on the Shroud of Turin—he has a swollen right cheek. Yet the prominent tuft of hair over the forehead here corresponds much better to a strikingly similar tuft of hair in earlier portraits of Christ in the East than the inverted "3" on the Shroud of Turin, which researchers have long assumed was the origin for that depiction. The inverted "3", however, does not in fact show a tuft of hair, as we know today, but rather is the

Detail from the fresco on the Via Sommeiller in Pinerolo with the sudarium *of Christ (above his shroud).*

mistaken attributions. This is the only cloth that one can realistically imagine being shown to the populace by a bishop on the city wall after it was rediscovered in Edessa in the year 544. And when all is said and done, only the "wondrously fair face" on this veil can reasonably be identified with the image about which a sixth-century writer still recounted that the "immaculate Virgin ... stretched the image out to the east and prayed before it" whenever she wanted to venerate her Son. Who, having seen this image on the veil, can still imagine that in these two instances the cloth in question could have been the gigantic sheet of the *sindon*?

On the pilgrimage of the shroud, therefore, Pinerolo holds a key position today. For many riddles concerning the shroud, it is a fork in the road. Indeed, from this location the path leads onward, but not only to Turin, because the fresco on the Via Sommeiller shows that in 1578 it was still understood that there were at least two cloths that are necessary and extremely helpful for a comprehensive description of the Shroud of Turin. There are two cloths, which are basically complementary, explaining and enriching one another, and they belong together, as they did in that first hour in Christ's tomb, when John also spoke explicitly about cloths and a separate *sudarium* or napkin. At least two witnesses were necessary in a Jewish trial in order to testify credibly that alleged facts were true. Once Jesus himself, in his debates with the scribes, said, "In your law it is written that the testimony of two men is true" [Jn 8:17]. (Therefore, not only does he bear witness to himself, but the Father who sent him also bears witness to him.) There were two men in dazzling apparel who greeted the women on that first Easter morning in Jerusalem in or in front of the tomb. There were two messengers. There were two cloths, then and now. Yes, two witnesses were

bloodstain from a wound on Christ's forehead that comes from the crown of thorns worn by the "King of the Jews". Only this *sudarium* can be the ancient *mandylion*—not the shroud. Very clearly delineated on it also are the "four folds" repeatedly mentioned in the first centuries in descriptions of a mysterious original image of Christ. By its sheer presence the little cloth corrects an immense number of required: that is why Peter and John had to run together to the tomb early that morning. And there were also precisely two cloths, not one, before the most intimate and precious treasure of the early Christian community was carried away from Jerusalem (together or separately?). We do not know how long they were together on their journey through time. That is why in the first millennium they are also so difficult to identify. Here a citation refers to the one cloth, there to the other. Therefore, along the way the names of the two become confused.

In the year 1157 the Danish abbot Nicholas Bergthorson described how, at the court of Manuel I Comnenus, in the chapel of the imperial palace in Constantinople (Byzantium), two relics from Christ's tomb were shown to him, not one: a burial cloth and a portrait. No one can say what relics these were and precisely what they showed. The same is true for almost all the early representations of Christ from the Byzantine East. There is no mathematical precision or order in this matter. Obviously, though, the clear depiction on the *soudarion* was generally known much earlier, because its origin in the tomb was less or not at all apparent. Only one thing is clear: there were different cloths and images from Christ's tomb at the beginning, and they exist today—and there was still an awareness of the connection between these cloths when the *Santa Sindone* was brought to Italy. But this awareness was then lost for around five hundred years, at approximately the same time that Christ's *sudarium* disappeared again from Rome and history loses track of it. Only recently did it come to light again, solving many riddles now and giving rise to new conundrums.

For only a few years ago did we learn again that the *Sanctum Sudarium* had been hidden and locked up since the seventeenth century in the side chapel of a little church dedicated

The sudarium *of Christ in Manoppello in the Abruzzi region has four distinct "folds", by which it was identified as early as the sixth century.*

Next spread: Fresco over the right side entrance of the cathedral in Pinerolo, in front of which the shroud was displayed in 1578, just before its final arrival in Turin.

to Saint Michael not far from the Adriatic coast, where it saw the light of day only twice a year, when it was brought out for two processions. Only in the past century was a new place assigned to it over the tabernacle on the high altar. And only around fourteen years ago did Father Germano Franco di Pietro, then the guardian of the Capuchin Friars, finally remove completely the veil behind which under normal circumstances it had continued to be hidden until then. The *sudarium* has come into

view again only in our time, after lying dormant like Sleeping Beauty for five hundred years—after the image of the large burial cloth had been impressed like a seal upon the collective imagination of Christendom during the last hundred years. At the last exhibition in Turin in the year 2000, apart from the populace of Manoppello, a few pilgrims and a handful of experts, hardly anyone knew about the *Volto Santo* [Holy Face] of Manoppello. Pope Benedict XVI changed that radically and irreversibly with his visit on September 1, 2006.

Yet, as we said, how the napkin was brought to Manoppello, at about the same time the shroud came to Turin, we do not know, despite much speculation and a legend that is difficult to believe. It was probably not mere robbers. The very name of the little town hints mysteriously at it. In the encyclopedia of Johann Heinrich Zedler from the year 1730, *manipulus* is translated as "a handful". That is why the coat of arms of Manoppello shows a hand full of ears of grain. But besides that, in the same old lexicon, we read that *manipulus* also means "a *sudarium* [napkin] with which one cleaned the vessels in the Christian church". That is why "among the clerics in the ancient Church, *sudarium* was synonymous with *mappula*."

I could hardly believe my eyes when I read the lexicon entry for the first time last summer. For of course, the "maniple" was the little "extra stole" that every Catholic priest in my childhood still had to wear over his left arm when celebrating Mass! It had never occurred to me that it was originally supposed to be a "sweat cloth" or a handkerchief. I would have never dreamed that sweat cloths could have assumed a place in the liturgy for many centuries—even though the tablecloth formerly spread over Christian altars could almost be a reminder of the Shroud of Turin. Nevertheless, the discovery cannot have anything to do with

the name of the little town of Manoppello. The name existed long before the veil arrived there. The founding of Manoppello goes back to Roman times. "But"—arguing the other way around—"might the napkin perhaps have been brought there on account of the name?" my wife asked, when I told her about it. "What?" I asked in reply. "Clearly the city was not named after the cloth, but isn't it possible that the cloth was brought to a place where, the messengers perhaps hoped, its name would remind people in later times about the *sudarium* of Christ?"

I had to laugh. For now I remembered how years ago someone in the gold city of Pforzheim told me the story that after the last war many inhabitants of Pforzheim did not find again the chests of gold that they had buried in their yards before the bombing started. They had not been stolen. The owners had just forgotten that gold is heavier than common soil and that therefore over the years—unless it was resting on a stone foundation—it gradually sank deeper and deeper into the earth, never to be seen again. Only those who had secured their chests with chains to a tree found their treasures again afterward. "Can it be, and do you perhaps mean," I asked my wife, "that the pious thieves of the little burial cloth intended to tie this treasure in the wilderness of the Abruzzi hills to this name, Manipulus, just as the wiser men of Pforzheim tied their chests of gold to a strong tree?" So that later on, in safer times, it could be found again? That by this choice of location in the wilderness of the Abruzzi hills the robbers intended to scratch

Reemerging from the mist of history: Manoppello in the Abruzzi hills, where the sudarium *of Christ has been preserved for over four hundred years.*

onto the map, so to speak, secret directions to lead future pious treasure hunters to the hidden crown relic of Christendom? That they intended thereby to provide a coded treasure map, like a pirate on a South Sea island for his buried chest of ducats? For in their time it was probably unimaginable that this treasure could ever be forgotten. "Isn't that a bit over-ingenious?" my wife then asked me. "Wild speculation, at least? It sounds perplexing. But who would ever claim to be able to prove such a connection?"

Now she is right again too. All this, of course, is just pure speculation and nothing else. That is why, having recalled the matter, we should let it rest there, because we still have to travel farther, to Turin at last, and also to visit the man who first discovered the inner connection between the two cloths for our time, so as to smooth the path for Benedict XVI back to the face of God in the countenance of Jesus—and that is not speculation at all. This man was Domenico da Cese, a colossal Capuchin who long ago deserved to have a book written about him. He too suffered with Christ's wounds, like his stigmatized confrere Padre Pio. He was born in 1905 and in 1965 was sent off by the province of his religious order to the obscure town of Manoppello, where at the age of sixty he fell in love with the veil and allowed himself to be seduced by it like a young girl who falls under the spell of the penetrating glance of the love of her life. He prayed day and night before the image, more and more enraptured by it.

In 1977, at the eucharistic congress in Pescara, for which Pope Paul VI traveled from Rome to the Abruzzi region, he then organized in the Adriatic port city an exhibition of the finely woven veil, with expensive, large-format photos that for the first time carried news of the existence of the *sudarium* beyond

the city limits of Manoppello. It is difficult to tell whether the pope saw the exhibition. Certainly, however, Renzo Allegri, an Italian journalist from Verona, visited the exhibition, for his report about it appeared in the December 1978 issue of the Swiss periodical *Das Zeichen Mariens* [Mary's sign].

In 1979 this article was finally pushed under the door of the cell of a certain Sister Blandina Paschalis Schlömer in the Trappist monastery Maria Frieden in the Eifel region; shortly afterward it was as if the heavy stone sealing the tomb of Christ were being rolled aside once more. For although Sister Blandina as a Trappist nun had vowed strict silence to this same Lord and to her religious superior, she could no longer hold her tongue afterward. She had to tell about it, and she did tell about it, and she moved to Manoppello as a hermit and told and told about it and did not stop until Benedict XVI finally, in response to her tireless talk, silently knelt in prayer before the *sudarium* in Manoppello. The rest is history.

Father Domenico did not live to see all this. Because he had a prophetic premonition that the face in Manoppello and the dead man on the Shroud of Turin were one and the same, he had set out on September 12, 1978, with one Signor Chionni di Rieti, from the Abruzzi hills to Turin, to the next-to-last exhibition of the shroud in the last century. On the morning of September 13, he visited for the first time in his life the image of his Lord on the *Santa Sindone*. That afternoon he went once again to a church, and that evening, while crossing the Via Paolo Braccini in front of the house numbered 29, where relatives of his friends lived, he was struck less than a meter from the curb by a speeding Fiat 500 and was injured. Four days later, on September 17, 1978, he died in the hospital. Before that, Father Pietro from the convent in Manoppello had hurried to his sickbed; the same confrere brought his body afterward to Domenico's native village Cese near Avezzano. In early 2009 the process for his beatification was initiated by bishop Bruno Forte in Chieti. The records already show ten well-documented miracles resulting from his intercession. Many people who knew him personally and many who know his story already consider him a saint of the burial cloths of Turin and Manoppello. I was the only one who had never heard of him when I was in Turin the last time in 2002.

The Capuchin priest Domenico Petracca da Cese discovered the sudarium *of Christ for our time. On September 17, 1978, he died in an accident while on pilgrimage in Turin.*

VULTURES
CIRCLING
GOLGOTHA

The silver casket from 1694 in which the shroud of Christ was saved from the flames of the burning Basilica of Saint John the Baptist in Turin during the night of April 11–12, 1997.

I still remember as though it were only yesterday how I had the opportunity to see the shroud as part of a small group. In a top-secret operation that took place from June 20 to July 23, 2002, specialists had removed from the shroud completely, after more than four hundred years, all twenty-nine patches and a backing cloth made of Holland linen, which four nuns had sewn onto it in the spring of 1534 after the fire in the palace chapel in Chambéry. Professor Giuseppe Ghiberti, the authorized agent of the cardinal of Turin for the shroud, had invited us afterward to an exclusive initial private viewing of the restoration work. Only a handful of men and women were permitted then to get some idea of how the shroud would look in all future exhibitions.

The necessary removal of the patches and of the debris that had collected behind them had been carried out in the strictest confidence, because absolute secrecy was the surest protection for the shroud. Scarcely any other object in the world ranks so high on the list of terrorist targets. The operation took place in the unpretentious new sacristy next to the cathedral. The additional materials were carefully catalogued, sealed and stored securely for further research. In early 2008 a special firm once again took 1,650 high-resolution pictures of details from the entire fabric; evaluating them will take years. The appearance of the *sindon*, of course, was not changed thereby. The intervention that most affected the sensible appearance and our perception of the shroud in our time was surely the cleaning of the shroud in 2002. In the *Ostensione della Santa Sindone* [Exhibition of the Holy Shroud] in early 2010 it became apparent to pilgrims from all over the world. But then no one knew that yet. As part of the restoration, the back side of the shroud too was thoroughly examined, photographed, put under

the microscope and scanned for the first time. Such immense quantities of new data were obtained thereby that they will keep scientists busy for generations to come.

Previous to that, I had last seen the shroud in 1998 from a distance with binoculars during the solemn exhibition, observing it from a pew in the cathedral and trying to spy all the

Stylized depiction of the exhibition of the shroud in the year 1898 by the bishops of Fossano, Vercelli, Turin, Genoa and Aosta.

traces about which I had read earlier. One year before that, it had again been saved at the last minute from a fire that had transformed the chapel behind the main altar of the cathedral, where until then it had been preserved, into a blast furnace. Not one thread had been singed in the incident. And so it changed dramatically only in 2002.

Cardinal Poletto had invited us to Turin in order to "counteract all the rumors" that

had rained down on the entire globe by satellite from Italy in the weeks before. There had been talk of new, malicious and "irreparable damage" done to the unique relic, which the cardinal and other obscurantists in his circle of advisers would have to take responsibility for after their "so-called restoration" of an heirloom of world culture. Probably, the story went, any intervention would already be too late. Therefore, it was all the more urgent that the shroud should be taken away from the "Turin Taliban" immediately and placed under the authority of UNESCO. Best-selling author Ian Wilson, "extremely alarmed", traveled from Australia to Turin, along with John Jackson from Colorado and a hundred other colleagues and scientists from Italy and the rest of the world. I had a whole stack of articles with news of the atrocity in my baggage, and now the shroud at this latest encounter was more beautiful than I had ever seen it before. The old patches had simply been removed along with the final traces of the fire. That was all.

But how lucid it had suddenly become in the process! I bent over the table, put my hand over my heart, had no idea what to do with my hands, eyes, feet and thoughts, walked from left to right, in front of the table and behind the table, and suddenly had forgotten everything that I knew about the shroud. I simply stood there enthralled by the tremendous impact and reality of the ancient fabric, which between all the burnt spots and stains lay there so unbelievably intact in front of me on the large table, preserved in excellent

Devotional picture in an eighteenth-century missal showing Christ being taken down from the cross and laid in the tomb, inspired by a miniature painted by Girolamo della Rovere.

condition. How delicate and pale the figure on the fine linen was in my memory, and how clear it was now! Without all the patches, the "shadow of the Lamb" now seemed to lie there as naked as Jesus who once lay in it, injured just as he was, with open wounds and no bandages. It seemed to me as though the wounds of the cloth too were now recounting the wounds of the dead man who had once been laid on it yet were transfigured, in repose, with a relaxed beauty, as a true image whose presence no human being can explain. Yet how could it be that it shows so few signs of moldering? I asked Mechthild Flury-Lemberg from Bern, who was responsible for the conservation operation. "Because it has no areas of decomposition", she answered. "Ancient cloths that have been preserved generally come from tombs. That is why they are also frequently decayed, often with large areas of rot. The man who was wrapped in this cloth, however, was not decayed."

I looked at the famous researcher inquisitively and then bent down again over the shadow of the slender fingers of that "man who was wrapped in this cloth", and the star-shaped traces of the flow of blood around the wound on his right hand and on the lower arm. Yes, the bloodstain on the right side of his chest is really so big that you could put half your hand into the open wound that the shroud once covered at that spot. And now the stain, observed from up close, suddenly appeared so small, so peaceful, pale violet, or pink, now that the wound just stops at the old burn mark and no patch covers the source anymore. The face of Jesus with his eyes closed lit up softly as I bent over it once more to say farewell; it left me speechless.

Was this not farewell forever? I certainly would not still be around for the next exhibition, I thought. Once again, silence filled the

Silk standard of the flagship of the house of Savoy in the Battle of Lepanto on October 7, 1571, with a depiction of the shroud (in the sacristy of the Dominican church in Turin).

draped room. Then all I heard was my heart beating as I clumsily helped the sacristan to unroll the claret-colored velvet cover back over the new sarcophagus made out of bulletproof glass, the darkness of which would again take in the most precious relic of Christendom for years to come.

VULTURES CIRCLING GOLGOTHA

From either side guards pushed a steel vault over the transparent display case, covered the shrine with a brocade tapestry, closed again the dark red curtains beneath the gallery of the Savoy kings, slid the double door of bulletproof glass in front of the side chapel and placed two large bouquets of roses to the right and the left in front of the marble balustrade, as we left the cordoned-off cathedral at around noon that Saturday as though after a funeral, although of course without any mourning. Only the pounding heartbeat, which did not subside for a long time.

I had never before come so close to the shroud and that image of Christ made out of blood, watermarks and faint shadows, which has kept minds in an uproar for hundreds of years—especially since it has also become an object of laboratory research and of debates at academic conferences. But if my sources are correct, no one yet has come to believe in Christ as the Son of the living God because of the discovery of a further indication of the authenticity of the shroud of Jesus, no matter how compelling the "proof" might be. Nor do I know of any case of a man or a woman ever falling away from that same belief on account of the surprising discovery of another bit of counterevidence. Nevertheless, the shroud is debated with bizarre fervor. Viewed dispassionately, one can only marvel at it. Yet somehow the shroud leaves few people dispassionate and almost no one who comes close to it cold. For some is it perhaps the fear that the skyscraper of science could collapse if someday even the genetic code of "this man" should be deciphered as well? Does the enigmatic appearance on the shroud perhaps—after all the questions that we may have about it—conversely pose to us the questions: Who are we, where do we come from and where are we going? Who wants to know? Obviously, the

spheres and levels of faith and science overlap in this "object" in a way that we find hardly anywhere else. Yet that does not explain the often childish willfulness of renowned professors or the moving obstinacy of highly qualified scientists, the zeal with which they argue again and again about the simple question of whether the shroud is genuine and true or not. Indeed, the answer lies beyond all controversy. Actually, they all could be calmer about it. But that is not the way it is; quite the contrary. The shroud breathes and really reflects a peace unlike that of any painting, yet strife and discord flutter about it like ravens and vultures around an old gallows—along with a unique culture of suspicion, insinuations, defamation and distortions. Around the shroud, spooky things often happen.

For the strife does not just divide people into one party in favor and one against; it even divides those who love the shroud among themselves, almost more so. For ages, Turin has had the highest concentration of witches and sorcerers in the whole peninsula and therefore more exorcists also than any other Italian city. When we—that is, Ellen, the best of all wives, and I—now finally returned to this beautiful city on the Po River and, on the evening after our long drive on the Via Milano, were enjoying a wonderful dinner with a bottle of Barolo, suddenly, even before dessert, we got into an argument the likes of which we had not experienced for years. Later on, neither of us could tease out, not even with tweezers, what it was actually about. We no longer even know what triggered it. There was simply no reason, and it was just horrible: fighting and bickering by such an old married couple as we were! For almost twenty-four hours we scarcely spoke a word. That is what things looked like initially at the end of our pilgrimage to the shroud of our Lord and Redeemer.

A "crown of thorns" like the one that was pressed onto the head of Jesus of Nazareth before his crucifixion, according to findings on the Shroud of Turin (Museum of the Holy Shroud in Turin).

It was dreadful, even crazy. I know that earlier, during the aperitif at the table, we had made fun of the "kindergarten" that many disputes about the shroud reminded us of. We had joked also about the rationally inexplicable zeal with which many "sindonologists" (as proponents of the interdisciplinary study of the great shroud call themselves) had protested and engaged in polemics against the discovery of the little napkin in Manoppello. Not one of them had welcomed the courageous move by the new pope in visiting Manoppello. Of course, it must have irritated people who for many long years had been building big, ambitious intellectual constructs to decipher the large shroud. A few had even proceeded to write caustic protests against the acknowledgment of the little veil; others started intrigues about

which we had reliable knowledge. No pilgrim had set out for the Abruzzi hills so lovingly, with such eager piety, as Domenico da Cese around thirty years earlier, although in the opposite direction, before he was run over by a Fiat 500 on September 12, 1978, here [in Turin, headquarters of Fiat] on the Via Braccini. Nor has a movement begun since then to make a little pilgrimage in caravans of Fiats to see the little burial cloth, despite the fact that the two places are only 726 kilometers [450 miles] distant—six hours and forty minutes according to the navigation system, the ideal day trip. Not to mention plans or initiatives to become spiritual sister cities. Instead, the competition that had suddenly cropped up was somewhat reminiscent of the misgivings of the bishop of Troyes, who in 1389 had protested so vehemently against the existence of the shroud and the exhibition of it in Lirey.

"What are, actually, the main arguments of those in Turin who are opposed to the little *sudarium* from Rome?" Ellen asked while we were still on the antipasto. "What can the people in Turin possibly have against it? Doesn't it correspond exactly to John's Gospel? What's more, without this *sudarium*, everyone should have noticed long ago that something was lacking in the large burial cloth."

"Right", I said, and poured some more wine. "Some say that it is painted. And all of them say it has not yet been studied sufficiently—that it is still much too risky and that therefore it is simply crazy to take it seriously."

"Ha!" My wife laughed with malicious irony, as only she can. "Has the *Santa Sindone* then become more authentic, genuine and true because of all the research? Or was the shroud perhaps less genuine in 1897, before the first photos and all the investigations? And maybe they were not entirely 'with it', all those people who in 1750 or 1850 were already convinced that they were dealing here with the genuine shroud of Christ? And can the napkin therefore have become less authentic because it spent the last few centuries tucked away like Sleeping Beauty? But that is a joke! No one has to believe in the burial cloths, but that argument is stupid."

Yes, all that was true. Perhaps Ellen's zeal should have startled me, since she otherwise usually leaves that to me. For as I said, it was unfortunately the last laugh that I remember that evening. It has been ages now since we have had a quarrel like the one in Turin. And the next day was not the sort that could put us in a better mood.

What was the matter? Doors [*Türen*] here that used to be wide open were closed to me this time. Many times when I dialed a telephone number, the person hung up as soon as I said my name. It must have acquired a miserable reputation here in Turin since I published a book some years ago about my initial research into the *sudarium* of Manoppello. Others turned their cell phones off. The most important contact to me, of course, is Professor Giuseppe Ghiberti, who was extremely helpful to me twelve years ago and again eight years ago. For that I remain eternally grateful to him. The very fact of my last encounter with the *sindon* I owe entirely to him, my farewell to the restored shroud, which would be presented to the world only later, in early 2010. I still find that moving.

The monsignor with the short gray hair is the most important adviser to the cardinal of Turin on matters concerning the relic, and very few people before him have been as familiar with the cloth. He plays a key role in all decisions affecting the shroud. We think very highly of him and are acquainted with him from Munich, Turin and Rome, from the cathedral, from pubs, at his house or at home with us, and I do not know where he was friendlier. Only now he unfortunately no longer has any time to welcome me.

Medallion with Christ's sudarium *at the head end of the old silver casket for his shroud in Turin (dated 1694, in the Museum of the Holy Shroud).*

THE "MISSING LINK" OF EASTER NIGHT

Negative of the face of Jesus on the first photo of the Shroud of Turin, taken May 28, 1898, by Secondo Pia (from the monastery church of Saint-Hippolyte-sur-Doubs).

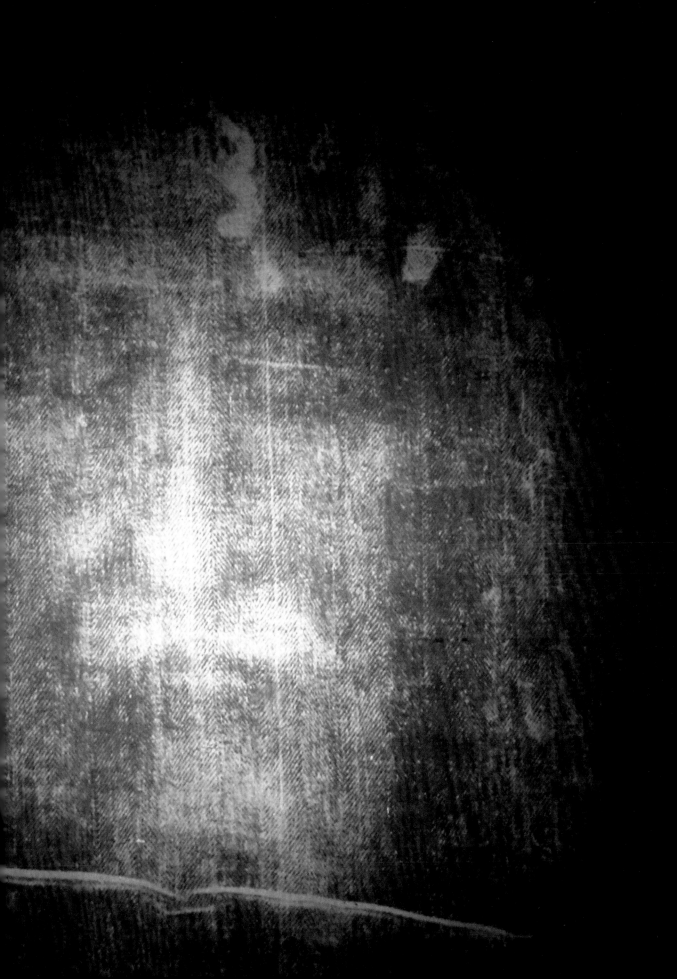

Entrance to the Church of the Holy Sepulcher in the Old City of Jerusalem, which is revered by the Greeks as the church of the Resurrection.

The shroud of Christ is still found today in the Duomo di Torino [cathedral of Turin], at the front and to the left in its heavily secured special cabinet behind bulletproof glass in the side chapel where in autumn of 2002 I had the privilege of bending one last time over the "bleeding head so wounded". I still can almost hear my heart beating then, practically in my throat, as I drew near to the tender countenance for the duration of a breath. Since then, the high-security sarcophagus has been locked again day and night. A bundle of thorns decorates the casket, and also a purple stole with a cross and three nails and the Latin inscription TUAM SINDONEM VENERAMUR, DOMINE, ET TUAM RECOLIMUS PASSIONEM. "We venerate your Shroud, O Lord, and contemplate your sufferings!" Faintly illuminated, a sepia-toned negative of the face on the shroud floats above and behind it, in front of a heavy red curtain the color of Bordeaux wine. Normally no one today comes any closer than that to the shroud.

Nevertheless, Turin is naturally full of traces of it. Beside copes made of royal purple, next to golden, shimmering, brocaded vestments and other precious ecclesiastical hangings, we find—not far from the cathedral—in a side room of the sacristy of the Dominican church, for example, a large old silk banner in a glass display case, on which the Mother of God is depicted in the middle with angels, unrolling the large burial cloth of Christ in front of the noonday sun. PROTECTOR NOSTER, ASPICE DEUS, ET RESPICE IN FACIEM CHRISTI TUI is embroidered in Latin all around at the edges. The psalm verse (Psalm 83:10 Vulgate) in English reads, "Behold, O God, our protector, and look on the face of thy Christ [here on our coat of arms]" (Douay-Rheims). This was the flag that flew on the main mast of the Savoy flagship as the united fleet of Western Christendom sailed in the bay of Lepanto against vastly superior Ottoman naval forces of Ali Pasha. That one day was decisive for Europe; in the evening the greatest sea battle of all time ended with an utterly astounding victory for the West. The flag is the so-called *Lepantina*, from the time when the Savoys still resided with the Holy shroud in Chambéry beyond the Alps.

Ten minutes further on, on the Via Domenico, anyone who has been following the pilgrimage of the linen cloth finds next door to the Church of the Fraternity of the Holy shroud a museum with a wealth of objects that have accompanied the *Santa Sindone* in recent centuries: old books, folio volumes, medallions, paintings, embroideries, a freshly woven crown of thorns, the cedar chest inlaid with flaking tortoiseshell in which it was carried across the Alps to Turin, the crimson panel of cloth in which it had formerly been rolled up. Brocade with pearls and gold embroidery covers the large silver casket in which the shroud was rescued in April 1997 from the burning cathedral, with magnificent enamel work all around. At either end of the treasure chest

there is a medallion imprinted with the face of Christ on the little napkin, clearly depicted with open eyes. Next to it, in the dusky shadows where you scarcely notice it, in another display case rests the bulky wooden box with which the attorney Secondo Pia produced the first usable photo of the Holy shroud a hundred years ago, on May 28, 1898.

At that time the picture immediately became world famous, and the story of how it came about has been told many times already. *Dottore* Pia had a passionate interest in the new medium and became one of the first amateur photographers. Portraits of the photographer himself show him with one of those projecting mustaches that many men around the turn of the last century used to wear like antlers. Secondo Pia was also one of the first of his time to experiment in his photographs with light bulbs, which had been invented twenty years before in America. On the occasion of two anniversaries celebrated by the house of Savoy, in 1898 the shroud was once again solemnly exhibited for eight days. This provided the opportunity to produce, finally, the first photo of the *Santa Sindone*, in the name of the modern era. The order to do so was not given until the exhibition had already begun. On account of the crowds, such a photo could be made only at night, with his own equipment, two artificial lamps—which burned more brightly than a thousand candles—and a generator that was required for them in the cathedral, which did not yet have electricity. Consequently, it was quite hot during the complicated photo shoot, in which the photographer was assisted by a Father Salaro and a Lieutenant Fino. The heat allowed only a few minutes at a time under the cloth beneath which Secondo Pia tried to capture the delicate image through the viewfinder of the camera. The first attempt failed. So then, four days later and four days before the end of the exhibition, Secondo Pia climbed up again at nine-thirty in the evening onto the scaffolding, chose an exposure time of around twenty minutes under different lighting, and at around midnight started to develop the plates in the darkroom with his assistants. Only one shot was successful.

"My heart almost stood still", he later said about the moment in which he finally lifted the fifty-by-sixty-centimeter [twenty-by-twenty-four-inch] photographic plate out of the chemical bath and for the first time held it up against the weak red light of the darkroom. Suddenly the murdered man stood before him with all his wounds and the majesty of a king, who for the first time appeared positively to the observer in the negative. "The plate almost slipped out of my hand. I nearly broke it, so startled was I to see now the face of Jesus, as no one had seen it for nineteen hundred years." Two weeks later a newspaper in Genoa printed a first report of the discovery, which no one had heard about yet. On June 14, 1898, the *Corriere Nazionale* in Rome spread the news, and on June 15 *L'Osservatore Romano* of the Vatican.

The story of the shroud, as we said, did not begin then, because even before that, many people were thoroughly aware of what the cloth is all about. Earlier generations also knew who was depicted on the shroud. In 1898 there was in western Europe alone a whole garland of churches that had sheltered this linen cloth, from Lirey via Saint-Hippolyte, [to] Vercelli, Chambéry and Turin. In Rome there was even a special church for a copy of the image. This was the Chiesa del Santo Sudario on the Via del Sudario, next to the great Basilica of Saint Andrew. Yet the first photo of the shroud gave an incredible new stimulus to research. Moreover, during the night of May 28–29, 1898, in Turin, a remarkable chain of events

that had begun in Jerusalem came full circle.

After all, we must look for the beginning of the story of the shroud in a "darkroom" too. That room still exists today, although in the year 1009 Caliph al-Hakim had it razed to its foundations and burned to quicklime. Yet later, the structure was completely rebuilt as it had been before. It is Christ's sepulcher in Jerusalem, where every morning the eyewitness Gospel of John about the Resurrection of Christ from the dead is read anew. It is the decisive passage of the Gospel for all Christendom. Therefore, it is also absolutely unthinkable that John could have lingered over trivialities in this passage. In any case, I have never heard any Gospel reading more often than these first eight verses from chapter 20 of John. Here I heard it in many languages, and even when I did not know one of them, no translation was necessary. For I already knew the text practically by heart during those two years in which, as often as possible, I walked early in the morning to that room. That was in the years of the last intifada, when it was as lonely and peaceful here as in the heart of Paradise. The room drew me like a magnet.

Therefore, I could still draw the chamber with my eyes closed: the low entrance; the stone bench along the right side; and in front of it, to the left, a passage so narrow that you can only kneel down in it diagonally. Christ's tomb was a so-called trough grave [*Troggrab*]; that is, the narrow passage to the left led into the chamber where, beside it on the right, the corpse, wrapped in cloths, was laid on the stone bank and left there. I still have in my ears the crackling of the candles from that room in which the spark of the Easter faith first came springing into the world, and we need only approach this hour closely enough—with this light of daybreak, with the Gospel of John and the cloths that he describes in it—and

The rebuilt chapel over the empty tomb of Christ in the interior of the rotunda, constructed by emperor Constantine, of the Church of the Holy Sepulcher, photographed early in the morning.

then we can still hear the crackling of this spark today. For indeed, *cloths* are what John speaks about most of all in his report of those moments; the Greek word *othonia* is a plural form. Therefore, there were several cloths that he saw lying there, in keeping with the Jewish burial rites that were customary then. Even a normal burial at that time required a series of cloths. The fact that the large *sindon* was among them goes without saying. Certainly among the cloths was also the bloodstained cloth that is preserved in Oviedo in northern Spain. It was pressed upon the face of the Crucified immediately after his death so as to collect the blood that came out of his mouth after his last breath. Surely it was buried with Jesus. Yet this cloth contains no image. There

are only bloodstains on it. Similarly, in Cahors in southern France, another bandage is preserved that was tied around Jesus' chin after his death to hold it up. This cloth too was buried with Jesus and likewise bears no image. The "image" on the Shroud of Turin, on the other hand, Peter could not possibly have seen or even unfolded already in the tomb. It was just much too dim inside. The chamber was also much too small for him to have unfolded it there. The shroud, after all, is four meters [thirteen feet] long. But the image of Christ is what makes the shroud inexplicably symbolic, not the bloodstains.

After mentioning "the linen cloths" twice, John speaks once again specifically about the "napkin, which had been on [Jesus'] head"

[Jn 20:5–7]. He describes its location with puzzling precision: the fact that it was "not lying with the linen cloths but rolled up in a place by itself". This *soudarion* was lying there by itself, separate from the other cloths. John attaches great importance thereto in this extremely concise text. If that was the case, however, it must have been lying on the ground. Otherwise there was no "place by itself" apart from the stone bench on the right side of the narrow passageway. Indeed, directly behind the bench, the bedrock wall projects straight upward. The bench is not a bed where something can disappear into a nook or cranny. The design of this particular sepulcher simply allows no other place "by itself" or "alongside"; its clear structure translates the position of the little cloth unambiguously from the text into reality. In this room, "not lying with the linen cloths" could only mean on the floor of the chamber, at the feet of the apostle Peter.

It is best if we set out afresh once again with him and John to Christ's tomb. Mary Magdalene had come running to them in the early morning, "while it was still dark" (!), and had breathlessly alerted them: "They have taken the Lord out of the tomb, and we do not know where they have laid him" [Jn 20:1,2]. Was this in an inn at the foot of the Mount of Olives or in lodgings on Mount Zion? We do not know. The way to Mount Zion would have taken around a quarter of an hour; to the Mount of Olives and back, at least twice as long. It would also have been more strenuous to go up the hill, through the city and around the city wall. That leaves you out of breath. Had Mary Magdalene already looked into the darkroom? She had seen in the dark that the stone had been rolled away from the tomb, John writes; now he was hurrying with Peter through the first light of dawn to the tomb. Had it become any brighter meanwhile? Quite possible, since daybreak in Jerusalem is a short process.

"Peter then came out with the other disciple, and they went toward the tomb", we read, at any rate. "They both ran, but the other disciple outran Peter and reached the tomb first; and stooping to look in, he saw the linen cloths lying there, but he did not go in. Then Simon Peter came, following him, and went into the tomb" [Jn 20:3–6]. John had to bend over. We can still see today how low the entrance was. There cannot have been all that much that he saw in the twilight of the chamber. But why did he not go in? Surely the nervousness of any pious Jew about graves played a role in it. After all, John had stood by the cross. He knew that Jesus was really dead. Simon Peter was nervous also and no less pious. But he was in an exceptional condition. Peter was beside himself after he had denied three times the person he loved most in his life two evenings before, in the hour of that person's greatest need. Now he came running belatedly and immediately went into the tomb. No commandment could have prevented him from doing so after the disturbing news from Mary Magdalene. He had to go in; he had to find out what had happened there.

It was not much. "He saw the linen cloths lying", John writes. Yet, without candles, without light except for the faint rays of dawn that fell through the low opening, we must unconditionally imagine this "seeing" in those moments as groping and feeling as well. What else? The cloths were ritually unclean, like the entire tomb in the first place, and it was as dark as a blackout, especially to the right near the entrance on the stone bench where Jesus had lain. So then Peter felt and "saw" the cloths, and it was immediately clear: HE was no longer there! There was no one left. He groped once again through the various empty cloths on the stone bench. Jesus was no longer lying in them. He was no longer there, no question about it!

Why did he not run out immediately to John and then with him to the Roman prefect? Why did he not exclaim also, "They have taken the Lord!" Why did he not dash off to the other apostles so as to consult with them about what they should do now, or to the Sanhedrin to shout, "You can't do that: first you kill our Master, and then you secretly get rid of him! He is still a Jew like you. Did he not have at least the right to rest in peace with the dead? What other outrage do you plan to commit?" Was he too afraid to do that? Why, then, did he not run with John to Joseph of Arimathea and Nicodemus, who had laid Jesus in the tomb and rolled the great stone in front of it? Why not? Why does the narrative now completely change course from Mary Magdalene and her realization, "They have taken the Lord out of the tomb, and we do not know where they have laid him"? Peter, after all, was not more intelligent, wiser or more prophetic than Mary Magdalene. Jesus could only have been carried off; what else? Maybe by Romans, maybe by robbers, by whomever: yet he was gone. No longer there. Simply gone. That is how the women had seen it, and so Peter too saw and felt it now—with just one difference.

For in his case, "he saw the linen cloths lying, and the napkin, which had been on [Jesus'] head, not lying with the linen cloths but rolled up in a place by itself" [Jn 20:6–7]. As we said, earlier it was still dark when Mary Magdalene was there. The entrance of the tomb faced east, toward the city wall. Now it was just beginning to brighten. Faint daylight fell through the opening of the rock into the little chamber. That was the difference.

For now Peter had suddenly glimpsed something else in the shadowy darkness on the floor. At his feet the light was caught in something indistinct, as the wind is caught in a shrub. Like a flicker from the burning bush. It shimmered golden, bronze. If it had been lying on the bench with the other cloths, the first rays of dawn would not have been able to lay hold of it; Peter would not have been able to see it or to feel it with his fingers, because it was so extremely fine. Only on the floor could it have been taken in by the light. No light at all fell on the bench—impossible. Because of the low entrance, the light could fall only on the floor. On the bench with the cloths, everything remained in the shadows. Only on the floor could Peter see something, and what he now saw there was delicate as woven breath and so fine that Peter would not have seen it either, had it been lying flat on the ground. Yet it was wrapped, tied, rolled, crumpled or folded up. The Greek verb *entylisso* that John uses can mean all these things. Thus, the expression makes just one thing clear: it was not lying there flat. It was a haze, but it must have been recognizable somehow as a "thing", as an "object" that caught the first rays of dawn. Naturally, Peter bent down and picked it up. It was the precious little cloth that had lain on Jesus' face, the finest sea silk. It was as light as an angel's feather as Peter picked it up, unfolded it and held it against the light of the entrance. What else? He must have held it that way, not toward the interior of the dark chamber, but up to the light. It was, however, a *cloth of light*. It reacts to light.

What Peter saw now in that tomb on the veil against the morning light made it in a blink of the eye as clear as the sun: no one had taken the Lord from the tomb. Jesus had not been stolen and carried away. Something completely new was in the world now. It was unheard of, what Peter glimpsed in the blue hours of the first Easter morning here, on that transparent fabric held against the light of the entrance. Here

suddenly Christ was looking at him! With open eyes! No man had ever seen this before. This cloth was "not made by human hands", as was said later. It was the true image. Three days earlier Peter had said that he did not know that man. Hours later he had had to watch from a distance and hear how Jesus, streaming with blood, cried out once again on the cross and died. Peter was still reeling from the shock—when now suddenly Christ himself looked out at him from the veil in his hand. Now he knew him. Now he recognized him immediately. "In thy light do we see light", Israel had read for centuries in the Book of Psalms [Ps 36:9]. Did that verse perhaps occur to him? Or did he already remember then the earlier intimations of Jesus that "the Son of man must ... be killed, and on the third day be raised" [Lk 9:22]? We do not know. Only one thing do we know. Besides the bewildering emptiness of the linens in the tomb, this message in pictures read: "I live." Jesus was no longer dead. The only thing corresponding to this image was not another image, no icon or other sort of portrait; the only thing corresponding to what he saw there was the living man.

It was unambiguous. Did he call John in afterward? Not necessarily. They were only two meters [yards] apart, one inside and the other outside the tomb. And so John noticed Peter's body language at the moment of his discovery. Then he too went inside, he adds in his Gospel, saying about himself: "He saw and believed" [Jn 20:8].

This John, however, was also "the disciple whom Jesus loved", as he was fond of

*"Here Christ rose, never to die again.
Here the history of humanity was
decisively changed." —Pope Benedict XVI
on his knees in the Holy Sepulchre in
Jerusalem, May 15, 2009*

emphasizing. He was the disciple who later took Mary, the Mother of Jesus, into his home (and Mary Magdalene as well, as we read several times in old sources) and thus drew from the Mother's sources for his so uniquely Marian Gospel. Was it therefore the love of Christ for him and his love for Christ that now made him perceive and understand the true image first? In any case, he does not say that Peter saw and believed. Can it be, then, that Peter was not the one who first lifted up the transparent veil and held it against the light and first saw the open, living eyes of the Risen One in the cloth, but rather John? Maybe. "The Risen One cannot be seen like a piece of wood or stone", Joseph Ratzinger wrote in 1985. "He can be seen only by the person to whom he reveals himself. And he reveals himself only to the one whom he can entrust with a mission. He does not reveal himself to curiosity but to love."[1]

Perhaps then it really was John, who in front of the entrance had allowed Peter to go first, who now first "saw and believed". After all, only John would also have been present at the burial and therefore would have known that "the napkin ... had been on [Jesus'] head." Only an eyewitness of the burial could know that. Or maybe not, since Mary Magdalene (or Mary, the Mother of Jesus) had surely told him later about all the details of the burial and how she had left the delicate sea silk over Jesus' face as a final salute. Had not Peter, in contrast, fled even before the crucifixion? (Indeed, he had denied Jesus three times even before Jesus was convicted.) He could hardly have known about the veil. In any case, though, John would have shown him the little cloth immediately, if

it was not the other way around. "For as yet they did not know the scripture, that he must rise from the dead", he continues afterward in the plural again [Jn 20:9]. One way or the other, it was all a matter of a few seconds.

Could it not be that all this happened quite differently? Not really, says anyone with common sense who takes the cloths and the texts of the Gospel seriously and is familiar with the tomb and its locale—and still has enough fingers to add one plus one plus one plus one plus one to make five. No, that is why I too say it very definitely after becoming, as chance would have it, the one human being on the face of the earth who in our time has been privileged to spend more time in the tomb in Jerusalem and in front of the *sudarium* in the Abruzzi region than anyone else. If you take the components together, therefore—the testimony of the eyewitness John, the place, the hour, the light and the cloths—if you take all that together, and add to it as the first thing, or the sixth, the Jewish dread of ritual impurity from graves, then by human reckoning it really cannot have been otherwise. Then for Peter in the tomb it must have been similar to what Secondo Pia experienced in Turin in the year 1898 with the first photographic plates of the shroud against the red light of the darkroom, only much more dramatic. In the tomb there must have been a visible sign of the incredible event of Easter night, and that cannot have been the missing body of Jesus. What Peter—or John—picked up in the tomb from the "place by itself" and held up to the light was the first commentary on what had happened there. To this day the little burial cloth complements the large burial cloth and makes it accessible. Together they fit into the Gospel of John like the last pieces of the puzzle.

For as we said, on the large burial cloth there was nothing to see at that first moment in the

[1] Joseph Ratzinger, *Seek That Which Is Above: Meditations through the Year*, trans. Graham Harrison, 2nd ed. (San Francisco: Ignatius Press, 2007), 90.

dark, narrow chamber where it could not even be unfolded. That brings us to the next step. For now we not only can but *must* observe how afterward Peter and John hastily gathered up all the cloths and brought them into the daylight. They had to bring them to safety. They must not allow anything else to go missing from this darkroom! Nothing could remain lying there. Who knew, then, what the other cloths concealed! Yet these are all secondary and tertiary considerations. For the moment they saw only this: death had lost its power in that room. The dead man was no longer dead; these cloths were no longer unclean. They could not possibly be. The irruption of Christianity into history began with a complete transformation. Had Christ not shown his face in the morning twilight on the *soudarion*, they would have left everything lying there. They were pious Jews, who do not take burial wrappings from empty tombs along with them. In the tradition of the Mishnah, Judaism is full of strict regulations that define the extreme uncleanness of anything even remotely connected with dead bodies and graves.

The Shroud of Turin, which shortly thereafter was already recounting the Passion of Christ in picture language to the original Christian community of Jerusalem—this linen cloth would therefore not have been salvaged without the little burial cloth in which the risen Lord showed his face. Mary Magdalene had left everything lying there and had run immediately to the apostles. Peter and John might have done the same. They might have left everything lying there, had this little cloth of light not alerted them. They might have simply dashed out. But as we said: the little cloth was there. Applied to the structure of the sepulcher, which has likewise been preserved, the image of light on the napkin is the "missing link" of Easter night, which encapsulates

a compelling logic concerning the course of all the actions and reactions of those few moments. Now they took it with them—and all the other cloths as well. This could be done only in secret, even early in the morning, and they brought the cloths not to the police but to Mary and the apostles. "Then the disciples went back to their homes", John writes [Jn 20:10]. Perhaps it was the inn on Mount Zion where four days earlier they had celebrated the Passover with Jesus, or maybe it was a cave dwelling in the Garden of Gethsemane, where they had found pilgrims' lodgings for the feast.

Yet "home", clearly, in those days meant not so much a house as the fellowship of the apostles with Mary. To them the cloths were brought first of all on Easter morning. In the midst of the original Christian community they became a priceless treasure. Were these

Late medieval epitaph at the side entrance of the Church of Saint Emmeram in Regensburg depicting Jesus risen from the dead emerging from the tomb with his facecloth.

not the first pages of the Good News about the Passion and Resurrection of Jesus Christ? Certainly they were! That is why, as we have already mentioned repeatedly, not only their origins but also their very existence had to be hushed up completely and concealed immediately. Since the first documents of the Gospel of the original Christian community had been composed on the most unclean scrolls imaginable for Jews in general, there could be no question of storing them anywhere but in the community's innermost secret room. Under no circumstances could the news be spread. Had knowledge about the existence of these burial cloths among the apostles in Jerusalem spread further—along with the apostles' ultimate violation of the commandments of ritual purity!—early Christianity and its first "home" would not have survived the scandal.

John nevertheless does not conceal the secret completely. Eight verses after his report on the cloths in the tomb, he is already recording in his Gospel that Jesus, on the evening of the first day of the week—"the doors being shut where the disciples were, for fear of the Jews" [Jn 20:19]—stood again in their midst with a peaceful greeting, breathed on each of them and showed them his wounds (which at that time had already been "inscribed" among them on the large burial cloth). "Fear of the Jews" alone could have prompted the disciples, who were themselves Jews one and all, to flee easily at that time to Bethlehem or to Gaza on the sea, or to the Jordan, to Jericho or into the hills of Galilee. In all those places they would have been safe. Instead, their "fear of the Jews", which on that first Sunday evening suddenly caused them to bar the doors, had no other reason than the surprising and dangerous new treasure in their midst. It is scarcely comprehensible otherwise. This was the so-called *arcanum* [closely guarded secret] of early Christianity, in which what was previously the most impure thing was suddenly revered as the purest of all. The light images of these cloths of light were immediately locked up so tightly under this code of secrecy that it was centuries before the news was released from that secret space—while the beautiful rumor of an image "not made by human hands" of God's countenance gradually filled the whole house of Christendom like incense.

View through the transparent sudarium *of Christ in Manoppello in the early dawn of September 7, 2009.*

LIGHT FOR
THE WAY
OUT OF
THE DESERT

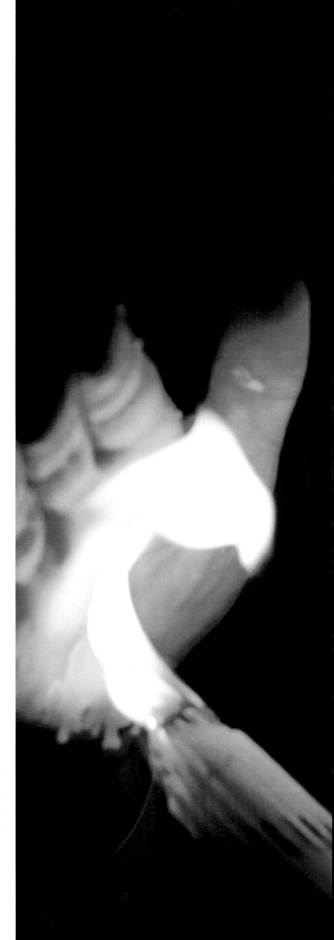

*Bundles of candles made up
of thirty-three slender candles
each in the hand of a monk at the
ceremony of the Easter miracle
of light in the Church of the
Holy Sepulcher in Jerusalem.*

The door to the crypt chapel is closed when the Greek patriarch has entered it without a lighter and matches.

And now something more. The memory, that is. First of all, of the enormous black beard of the powerfully built Greek monk with the ponytail who guarded the Holy Sepulcher during my time in Jerusalem (in the years 2000 and 2001). Then of his eyes, likewise black as briquettes but glowing even more when he defended the chamber against the claims of the Latins, against the Armenians, and of course against tourists and pilgrims. He watched rabidly to make sure that the status quo was observed and that the agreed-upon times for the liturgies of the various Churches in the Holy Sepulcher were kept to the minute. Inside the tomb, he extinguished the thin wax candles

that had been lit by the pilgrims and stuck in the bowl of sand, when there were too many of them. He took them in his hairy fist, blew them out, and at the same time with his left hand opened an icon of the Magdalene at the back wall like a cupboard door, so as throw the candles in carelessly against a charred wall of rock, to join other scraps that were still lying there, along with a plastic bottle. He liked me as he might a stray cat, because I was so often prowling around the old stonework. That is why he also informed me that that rock face behind the icon was the only remnant of the old rock tomb—all that was left of the original sepulcher complex (like the stump of a tooth in the old bedrock from which the tomb had once been hewn), after Caliph al-Hakim had ordered that the establishment be burned down. That was a thousand years ago now, in 1009 to be exact!

Anyone who knows a bit of art history can tell that the crypt chapel today, ornately clad with pink marble, is a Rococo creation of the eighteenth century. An earthquake had made this most recent new construction necessary. Nevertheless, the monk explained to me, all the old forms and dimensions of the original rock tomb had been carried over exactly. While the chapel today is only around three hundred years old, nevertheless its empty inner core still coincides with the interior of the old tomb in which Jesus—here, on this spot—had been laid after the crucifixion. "It was all here!" That is why the piece of charred rock face behind the hinged icon is the last material witness, he added, opening and closing once again the icon behind which his little junkroom was now located.

His name? I never asked about it, yet even today I could still paint his face and his imposing figure beneath the long black work apron that he usually had tied around him. One day, I watched him recount in detail, to a female American pilgrim who had asked him about it, how the Holy Fire comes about that the Greek patriarch lights every year at Easter in the crypt, always on Holy Saturday, at around two in the afternoon, in an ancient ceremony, without lighter, without matches, without burning candles, without anything, only "with light from heaven": a fire that the patriarch passes on to the faithful, who in no time turn the Church of the Holy Sepulcher into a sea of flames, as they have often told me. Year after year it is the heart of the Orthodox Easter celebrations in Jerusalem, for which the city is flooded with pilgrims, especially from Greece, from the islands and from Russia, with the old ladies dressed in black with their unshaven husbands, who often waited persistently for days in front of the Church of the Holy Sepulcher on little folding stools.

"Do you really mean to say that your patriarch lights the Paschal candle by a miracle?" I now asked the monk, dumbfounded after the lady who had just been hanging on his every word finally set him free again. Now his eyes glowed so ardently that even I could have lit a candle or a cigarette with them. "How could you ever think to doubt it", he hissed, shaking his head at me. "This fire falls one hundred percent from heaven. It is an absolutely supernatural process. This fire is not made by human hands!"

"Not made by human hands": back then I did not yet know the expression as I do today and would not have taken it so seriously either, especially since my friend Kevork from the Armenian Quarter later offered a second opinion explaining the same event. He winked at me incredulously over his glass of tea [as we sat] behind the Jaffa Gate, and he put his tongue in his cheek. How could anyone be so naïve? "Of course it is man-made", he said in English, grinning maliciously and snapping his lighter on. "Of course the fire is lit by a human hand!" He had learned this personally, firsthand, from the Armenian patriarch, and he, after all, is not just anybody. It goes without saying that he was never in the tomb together with the patriarch on that occasion. How could he be? No one has ever been with him at that moment. To date, no witness has ever been allowed to observe it. Yet he knew also that I considered him preeminently wily (in keeping with an old maxim in the Near East, according to which "every Armenian is as wily as ten Jews, and every Jew as wily as ten Greeks").

Kevork, however, was not only wily but also extremely helpful. That is why he made arrangements for me to be admitted to the Church of the Holy Sepulcher for the next liturgy of the Easter light. The place was again filled to the point of bursting, so that it was immediately obvious why nobody gets in without having connections. In the rotunda with the crypt chapel in the middle there was not enough room left to fit another sparrow. We were nailed to the spot, so to speak, pressed against one of the mighty pillars to the left in front of the entrance to the tomb. I had spent the night before on the roof of the church with the Ethiopians, the dark-skinned children of the queen of Sheba, who danced up there under the full moon like the ancient Jews, who three thousand years ago set out from Egypt, and whose singing sounded as though it were another thousand years older than that, perhaps from the days of Abraham. It was beyond time and space—and so it was now. The noise of the crowd was deafening, between the shouts, the crying children and the police whistles. It was one big uproar until finally the actual ceremony was introduced by a moving rendition of the *Kyrie eleison*: Lord, have mercy on us! Lord, have mercy on us! A loud "tock, tock, tock" announced in the suspenseful silence that the threefold procession of the patriarch around the tomb had begun. The Muslim guards of the Church of the Holy Sepulcher in their Ottoman uniforms opened the way for him, tapping their metal-reinforced shepherd's staffs rhythmically on the paving stones of the floor. Finally these noises too faded away into an eerie calm before the storm as the Greek patriarch Diodoros I with his snow-white beard removed all his splendid vestments and entered the tomb through a narrow alley. A guard closed the little double door after him until it snapped

shut. Silence. Breathless, murmuring silence. A minute passed, two, three, and suddenly a bolt of lightning. It was as though a spark from the burning bush had struck the church. In an instant, truly in a matter of seconds, the light that the patriarch held out at the door lit taper after taper and kindled overwhelming jubilation. In no time everyone was holding a burning candle in his hand, with a rapid decrease of oxygen in the magnificent space, light upon light, in one big ecstasy of joy. Now the crowd too dispersed from within. With tapers in hand, they all pushed their way outside. In front of the Stone of the Anointing in the atrium, a Russian woman handed me a burning bundle made up of thirty-three slender tapers, after first stroking the fire ecstatically over her face and body, through her hair and over the veil of her headdress. The flames did not singe and burn her hair or the veil any more than the fire of a burning thorn bush on Sinai had consumed the parched thicket before Moses' eyes. Yet her eyes were aglow. "Christos anesti! Christos anesti ek nekron! Alithos anesti!" Christ is risen! Risen from the dead! Truly he is risen! It was incredible.

Now, though, years later, I have suddenly gotten hold of a report of how Diodoros I himself, of all people—the patriarch whom I saw then—relates what actually happens when he enters the tomb. Back then I had not really taken the incident seriously; Kevork's winks reliably prevented that. But now suddenly I read in a report that was sent to me just yesterday from Germany that the patriarch is always searched before going into the tomb to check whether he has matches or a lighter on his person. He is allowed to take nothing with him except two unlit candles, and for this ceremony he wears only a simple white garment without pockets—he, who otherwise always makes his entrance into the church vested so

Above and on the next spread:
The unique ceremony of the "light not made by human hands" always takes place at the same time at two o'clock on Holy Saturday and goes back many centuries to the earliest liturgical recollections of Christian Jerusalem.

opulently, with such incredible splendor. The chamber was likewise carefully searched to make sure that no hidden sources of light had been concealed there beforehand. "I step into the tomb", he writes,

> and kneel down in holy fear before the stone bench on which Jesus was laid to rest after his death, from which he rose again from the dead. I find my way in the dark and fall on my knees. At this point I recite certain prayers that were handed down to us over the centuries, and I wait—sometimes a few minutes. But usually the miracle occurs right after the prayer. An indescribable light seeps from within the stone on which Jesus was laid. Normally it has a blue tint. But the color can change and assume many hues. Human words cannot describe it. The light ascends like mist from the sea. It almost looks as though the stone is surrounded by a cloud. But it is light. It behaves differently from one year to the next. Sometimes it covers only the stone. Other times it illumines the whole burial chamber, so that the people waiting in the church see the tomb full of light. It does not burn. In the sixteen years in which I have now been patriarch of Jerusalem, I have never yet burned my beard. The light has a different consistency from the fire that burns

in the oil lamps. At a particular point it rises up and forms a pillar, at which I can light my candle. After I have received the fire, I go out and give it to the Armenian patriarch, then to the Coptic patriarch and then to all the people who are in the church.

From this point on I myself am now an eyewitness. For I myself in turn have experienced it, with the explosion of light through the whole space and the ringing and tolling of the bells, which goes through the very marrow of your bones and seems that it will never stop, to proclaim the news of Christ's Resurrection from the dead and of the reappearance of the Holy Light to the city and to all the earth. All that was and is extremely, utterly real. The light that condensed into a little pillar reminded her, my wife said, of the pillar of fire in Sinai, in which God went before the Israelites at night and showed his people the way out of the desert into the Promised Land. But can we believe the patriarch at all? Doesn't the whole thing sound too fantastic? Who ever heard of such a thing?

I surf a little on the Internet and quickly find there the author of the interview with the patriarch. It is the Danish journalist Christian Hvidt, who recently became the first Catholic to qualify as a lecturer at the University of Copenhagen since the Reformation. Now he teaches at the Gregorian University. I could call him, but first I continue to read his report. "Every year, the miracle moves me again profoundly", the patriarch says in it. "We experience many miracles in our Church, and miracles are nothing strange to us. It often

From the light of the patriarch that is set aflame in Christ's tomb, the candles of all the pilgrims are ignited "at the speed of light".

happens that icons weep when heaven wants to show us that it is close to us. We also have saints to whom God grants many spiritual gifts. None of these miracles, however, has such an incisive significance for us as the miracle of the Holy Light. It is almost like a sacrament. It makes Christ's Resurrection present as if it had happened a few years ago." The ceremony of the "miracle of the Holy Fire" is "probably the oldest Christian ceremony in the world that has been celebrated unchanged", Hvidt then adds to the testimony of the prince of the Church.

Since the fourth century various sources are said to have reported again and again about its miraculous power. And in times when matches and lighters were as yet totally unthinkable, the process is repeatedly described in the same way, in the same place, at the same time, at the same hour and in the same liturgical space and framework. To the left of the main entrance to the Church of the Holy Sepulcher stands a pillar that is mysteriously cracked, and my wily Armenian friend once recounted for me the legend that the Holy Fire struck there directly out of that pillar when the Mamluks tried to forbid the Greeks to perform the ceremony of the miraculous fire. But can we simply trust such sources blindly? [On the other hand,] can we simply assume that the Greek patriarch and all his predecessors are liars? Or a series of charlatans?

The Greeks make up the most distinguished ecclesiastical community in Jerusalem: here we are dealing with the oldest Church in the world; it goes directly back to the original Christian community. Naturally, the Greeks are proud of this origin. It is understandable that the other Christians in Jerusalem—from the Armenians to the Copts and the "Latins"—have often envied them that status. The Greek patriarch is the direct descendant of James,

"the Lord's brother", the first bishop of the Holy City. Every name of his successors has been as reliably handed down by tradition as the names of the successors of the apostle Peter in Rome. Now, though, at any rate, I realize for the first time that back then I did not have the faintest idea of what I was actually attending. I had never experienced anything like it before. I simply did not know what I was witnessing during that Easter celebration in the year 2000. All of them knew about it, all the Greeks, all the Russians, all those ladies with their fire bundles (made out of thirty-three slender tapers bound together, corresponding to the number of years that Jesus lived); only I did not. What to think about the miraculous light and the blue fire from the tomb, I still do not know and cannot know. Yet the fact that here, where the spark of the Paschal faith came springing into the world, there is a special liturgy of light whose tradition goes back to the earliest period of Christianity—that is nothing but a plain fact.

The Paschal miracle of light is the climax of every pilgrimage from the Orthodox world to the oldest episcopal see in the world, by the sepulcher at the foot of the Golgotha rock.

LIGHT FOR THE WAY OUT OF THE DESERT

THE GOSPEL OF THE EARLY CHRISTIAN COMMUNITY

The account of Christ's Resurrection in Jerusalem in chapter 20 of the Gospel of John in a Lutheran Bible from Erfurt published in 1735.

heimlich aus furcht vor den Jü[
er mögte abnehmen den leichna[
Und Pilatus erlaubete es. Derow[
er, und nahm den leichnam JEfu
*Marc. 15, 43. 2c.

39. Es kam aber auch Nicode[
*vormals bey der nacht zu JEfu
war, und brachte † myrrhen und a[
ter einander, bey hundert pfunde[
*c. 3, 2. † Matth. 2, 11.

40. Da nahmen sie den leichna[
und bunden ihn in leinen tücher m[
reyen, wie die Jüden pflegen zu be[

41. Es war aber an der stätte, d[
creußiget ward, ein garten, und in[
ein neu grab, in welches niemand[
get war.

42. Daselbst hin legten sie JEf[
des rüsttags willen der Jüden, die[
grab nahe war.

Das 20. Capitel.

Christi auferstehung geoffenbaret, und[
get in Judäa.

1. AN *der sabbather einem komm[
ria Magdalena frühe, da e[
finster war, zum grabe, und siehet, [
stein vom grabe hinweg war.
*Matth. 28, 1. Marc. 16, 1. Luc. 2

2. Da läufft sie, und kommt zu Sim[
tro, und zu dem andern jünger, [
JEfus lieb hatte, und spricht zu [
Sie haben den HErrn weggenomm[
dem grabe, und wir wissen nicht, [
ihn hingelegt haben.

3. Da* ging Petrus und der ander [
hinaus, und kamen zum grabe. *Luc.

4. Es lieffen aber die zween mit e[
der, und der ander jünger lieff zuvor, [
ler denn Petrus, und kam am erste[
grabe,

5. Kucket hinein, und siehet die [

6. Da kam Simon Petrus ihm nach, und ging hinein in das grab, und siehet die leinen gelegt,

7. Und das schweißtuch, das JEsu um das haupt gebunden war, nicht bey die leinen gelegt, sondern beyseits eingewickelt, an einem sondern ort.

8. Da ging auch der andere jünger hinein, der am ersten zum grabe kam, und sahe, und gläubte es.

9. Denn sie wusten die schrift noch nicht, daß er von den todten auferstehen müste.

10. Da gingen die jünger wieder zusammen.

11. Maria aber stund vor dem grabe, und weinete draussen. Als sie nun weinete, kuckte sie in das grab,

12. Und siehet zween *engel in weissen kleidern sitzen, einen zun häupten, und den andern zun füssen, da sie den leichnam JEsu hingelegt hatten.   *Marc. 16,5. 2c.

13. Und dieselbigen sprachen zu ihr: Weib, was weinest du? Sie spricht zu ihnen: Sie haben meinen HErrn weggenommen, und ich weiß nicht, wo sie ihn hingelegt haben.

14. Und als sie das sagte, wandte sie sich zurück, und *siehet JEsum stehen, und weiß nicht, daß es JEsus ist.   *Matth. 28,9.

15. Spricht JEsus zu ihr: Weib, was weinest du? Wen suchest du? Sie meinet, es sey der gärtner, und spricht zu ihm: Herr, hast Du ihn weggetragen, so sage mir, wo hast du ihn hingelegt? so will Ich ihn holen.

16. Spricht JEsus zu ihr: Maria. Da wandte sie sich um, und spricht zu ihm: Rabbuni; das heisset, Meister.

17. Spricht JEsus zu ihr: Rühre mich nicht an, denn ich bin noch nicht aufgefahren

zu meinem Vater. Gehe aber hin zu meinen brüdern, und sage ihnen: Ich fahre auf zu meinem Vater, und zu eurem Vater, zu meinem GOtt, und zu eurem GOtt.   *Pf. 22,23. 2c.

18. *Maria Magdalena kommt, und verkündiget den jüngern: † Ich habe den HErrn gesehen, und solches hat er zu mir gesagt.   *Marc. 16,10. †1 Mos.32,30.

(Evang. am 1. sonntage nach ostern.)

19. AM *abend aber desselbigen sabbaths, da die jünger versamlet, und die thüren verschlossen waren, aus furcht vor den Jüden, kam JEsus, und trat mitten ein, und spricht zu ihnen: Friede sey mit euch.   *Luc. 24,36. 2c.

20. Und als er das sagte, *zeigete er ihnen die hände, und seine seite: Da wurden die jünger froh, daß sie den HErrn sahen.   *1 Joh. 1,1.

21. Da sprach JEsus abermal zu ihnen: Friede sey mit euch. Gleichwie *mich der Vater gesandt hat, so sende Ich euch.   *Jes. 61,1. Joh. 17,18.

22. Und da er das sagte, blies er sie an, und spricht zu ihnen: Nehmet hin den heiligen Geist.

23. *Welchen ihr die sünden erlasset, denen sind sie erlassen; und welchen ihr sie behaltet, denen sind sie behalten.   *Matth. 16,19. c. 18,10.

(Evangelium am St. Thomas-tage.)

24. THomas aber, der zwölfen einer, der da heisset Zwilling, war nicht bey ihnen, da JEsus kam.

25. Da sagten die andern jünger zu ihm: Wir haben den HErrn gesehen. Er aber sprach zu ihnen: Es sey denn, daß ich in seinen händen sehe die nägelmaal, und lege meinen finger in die nägelmaal, und lege meine hand in seine seite, will ichs nicht glauben.

26. Und über seine jünger ... nen: Komm... schlossen wa... spricht: Fr...

27. Darno... che deinen fi... de; und rei... sie in meine... sondern glä...

28. Thom... ihm: *Mei...

29. Sprich... mich gesehe... Selig sind... gläuben.

30. Auch ... sus vor sein... ben sind in d...

31. Diese a... gläubet, JE... tes, und da... ben habt in...

Christi auf...

I. DArna... mal d... Tiberias.

2. Es war... trus, und ... ling, und † ... lilä, und ... zween seiner...

3. Sprich... Ich will hi... zu ihm: S... Sie gingen... schiff alsoba... gen sie nicht...

4. Da es ...

Images not painted by human hands. Fire not kindled by human hands. Mysterious blue shining. A Paschal miracle of light that causes excitement in Greek Christendom year after year. Jesus and Mary! We were back in Rome again, sitting at the window and discussing in retrospect the long journeys that we had made in recent years. I had not noticed that I had fallen silent, yet the fact that the chamber at the very heart of Christendom, which I had imagined I knew so well, treasures the memory of Christ's Resurrection in two independent miracles of light, had probably left me speechless (for a moment)—along with the fact that I never made use of the opportunity to investigate the phenomenon more closely during my time in Jerusalem. How easily I too could have interviewed the Greek patriarch! For are we not really obliged to consider the empty tomb—and no other place, not even the Cenacle of the Last Supper—as the first home of Christendom? The little chamber in which a faint ray of light first gave Peter and John a clear picture of Jesus' Resurrection. The recapitulation of a plausible sequence of events in the empty tomb may perhaps be only a minuscule discovery, but it is quite close to the most important event in world history. After that, how could the tradition about the miracle of a Holy Light in the Holy Sepulcher not leave me bedazzled and astounded?

Why, though, does the miracle always take place on Holy Saturday at two in the afternoon and not at night, not at dawn? Does this mean perhaps that we would do better to imagine the specific act of Christ's Resurrection from the dead in the middle of the Sabbath, in other words, on the holiest day of Judaism, on which he had been warned countless times by his critics not to make a false move, including any miracles and healings? Who wants to know? Does the "Resurrection on the third day" mean then the *discovery* of the Resurrection? The discovery of the empty cloths? The discovery of the shining image? Of the dazzling images? Even the patriarch may not have been able to give me an exhaustive answer to that question. One thing, though, is clear: it is probably better for us to imagine the concrete Resurrection of Christ in space and time not as a leisurely stretch after a deep sleep but rather as an unprecedented, gripping intervention of God in history. And even after the catastrophe of the crucifixion, the apostles and the women at first observed the Sabbath strictly as pious Jews. But that was not necessarily the case with the Lord of the Sabbath. What better day, actually, could he have chosen for his Resurrection than his favorite day?

I heard Gregorian chant, as I so often had heard it and had sung along in the Church of the Holy Sepulcher: "Deum de Deo, lumen de lumine, Deum verum de Deo vero". I turned around. "Was that you?" I asked Ellen. "Did you just hum that beautiful passage from the Credo, 'God from God, Light from Light, true God from true God'?" No, she laughed, she had neither hummed nor sung it, although she herself had just been thinking that, in the oldest profession of faith in Christendom, light figures so prominently right at the beginning, precisely as if light were not merely an old honorific title for the Almighty but an expression of his essence. "Our custom of the Paschal fire in Europe must be dependent on that tradition, don't you think?" she now asked me. It is quite possible that this fire too is meant to keep alive the memory of the first light in the tomb, but

Vera Icon (True Image) by the Master of Hallein (ca. 1450), from Salzburg (in the Germanisches Nationalmuseum in Nürnberg).

Vera Icon with clear folds and a crown of thorns made of evergreen wood on the bottom of a box for storing corporals in the church of Bad Wimpfen, 1488.

of course I did not know for sure. In any case, it is stirring when the pope in Rome every year at the Easter Vigil lights the Paschal candle from the Paschal fire and with the threefold cry "Lumen Christi!" (Light of Christ) carries it into the darkened basilica and there lights everyone's candles with it—just like the patriarch in Jerusalem, in the first episcopal see of the world, at the foot of Golgotha.

"I am the light of the world" [Jn 8:12], Jesus had said there, in Jerusalem, to the Pharisees right at the beginning of his controversies with them. That was on the other side of the city, in the old Temple district—where he also reminded them that two witnesses are always necessary in order to testify credibly about a matter before Jewish tribunals. Is this not true also, though, of the testimony of the burial cloths, the large linen cloth and the small *sudarium*—which remarkably become one in the light that inscribed two different images of light on them?

THE GOSPEL OF THE EARLY CHRISTIAN COMMUNITY

"I don't know whether you can put it that way", Ellen said. It is clear, at any rate, that many ancient memories are still treasured up in the liturgy, through many generations of oblivion, and are only waiting there to be recalled someday. Thus, she cannot escape the suspicion that the large altar cloth at the old Mass in the Roman Rite, together with the *velum*, the little veil over the chalice, recall the secret treasure of the early Christian community, the *sindon* and the *soudarion* in its midst. Indeed, if we take the Gospel and the Sacrifice of the Mass seriously, the purpose of these cloths too, after all, is "to cover the Body and the Blood of Christ, and if need be to catch it, if the chalice should tip over and the Precious Blood be spilled."

"A marvelous observation", I said, and at the same time doubted this all-too-beautiful connection, however compelling the assumption of a mysterious flow of data through history via the liturgy may be. Yet Ellen's remark about the "early Christian community" had reminded me of something else. "Just a moment", I said, as I stood up and went into our small and unfortunately very disorderly library to look for *Das Evangelium der Urgemeinde*. A green paperback book! But I could not find it. I still knew half the contents by heart, though. Rudolf Pesch had written the book almost thirty years ago in Freiburg and thereby made a great impression on me. The renowned New Testament scholar claimed at that time—based on the Gospel of Mark, who was the companion of the apostle Peter—to have filtered out by painstaking detail work a self-contained text about thirty pages long that should be considered the foundational proclamation of the early Church—the "Gospel of the early Christian community", as Pesch called it in the title. It was an eyewitness report, as he maintained, that had been composed less than five years after Jesus' death, in which the story of his ascent to Jerusalem, his final days, his arrest at night and his condemnation to death on the hill of criminals outside the city gates was recounted. I cannot really evaluate the analysis, but I trusted it then, as I did many other scholarly findings; indeed, in such matters we usually depend on our trust in this or that scholar and in the reliability and seriousness of his methods.

Yet the title of this study—*The Gospel of the Early Christian Community*—was bold and ingenious; I myself can judge that. For it must have existed at one time: a proto-Gospel, so to speak, a vital core of all the written records and proclamations concerning the events in Jerusalem and the life, the Passion and the Resurrection of Jesus Christ. It could not have been otherwise. Every tradition has such a center. The center of the Gospels—the true pillar of fire, the blue flame from which its Holy Light was kindled—is naturally Jesus of Nazareth. The first pages of these Gospels, however, I know today, cannot have been a text that can be filtered out of one or another of the Gospels. The first pages of the Gospels were not written down five or ten or twenty years after Jesus' death either but rather on that first Easter night. The first pages of the Gospels are the two messages in picture language from the tomb. The hieroglyphics of these two cloths were the very first to recount the true Gospel of the early Christian community.

No other document can claim this status. The great shroud in Turin with the traces of the Passion is the first page of the Gospels. The delicate little napkin, which was revered for so long in Rome as "the veil of Veronica of Jerusalem", is the second. Both originate at the zero hour of Christianity. Thus, two images—and not any new scrolls—form the hot core of the Good News of Christendom. The images were there when words failed—and the apostles were still speechless. These cloths were the first, and then came the stories that the women and the apostles told among themselves about that Easter night; the written accounts that we call Gospels came only much later. Any other sequence of events is quite unthinkable. These two cloths made up the Gospel of the early Christian community.

That may sound absurd, but there is no other way of thinking about it if we—once again—add one and one to make two and take seriously the Easter Gospel of John and these cloths and regard them as authentic. At the beginning of Christianity, therefore, there was not a sort of original written source about the truths that Jesus spoke and the miracles that he worked. That could not have powered the liftoff of a world religion. At the beginning of the Church stands what he suffered and what he looked like. No words at that beginning but rather two original images recounted that the Resurrection is real and that death since then is only a shadow of its former self. Life is life. Death is a shadow. Love is life. Or, as Thornton Wilder wrote roughly two thousand years later in his novel *The Bridge of San Luis Rey*: "There is a land of the living and a land of the dead and the bridge is love, the only survival, the only meaning." That is found also in these two images. They are one single love letter, and there is absolutely nothing in them that contradicts the statements in the Gospels. They do not contradict the Sermon on the Mount, and they do not contradict what is said about the Crucified One, who two nights and three days after his death showed himself alive again to the living.

The shroud in Turin still depicts the majesty of the "King of the Jews" in Old Testament terms, so to speak, as a silent priest; the napkin in the Abruzzi hills shows him, in contrast,

already as the Messiah, as the "Holy One of Israel" to whom the prophets had stretched out their hands.

In Judaism linen was used for priestly garments, while precious byssus, the mussel-anchor silk of the napkin, was reserved for the splendid vestments of the high priest. Byssus is also the most prominent material in the last book of the Bible, the mysterious Revelation of John. The two cloths therefore depict in a mysterious way the two natures of Christ, the human, mortal body as well as his everlasting, incorruptible divine nature. On the one "image" we see that he was scourged. Gigantic nails were driven through his wrists and feet—one nail for both feet, one over the other (the Romans were of a practical turn of mind and frugal). He had literally sweat blood. He was "crowned" with thorns. He had received a heavy blow to the face. He had fallen on his nose. His side was "pierced" and—truly—"blood and water" came forth from the wound [Jn 19:34]. That can still be read from the indications here. The man was dead. And here he lies stretched out as "the Servant of God" before our eyes, as Isaiah had sung about him more than seven hundred years earlier in words that were inscribed here once again in picture language:

> There was in him no stately bearing
>   to make us look at him,
> nor appearance that would attract
>   us to him.
> He was spurned and avoided by
>   men,
> a man of suffering, accustomed to
>   infirmity,

Vera Icon on the napkin of the Flemish "Master of Flémalle" (1375–1440) in the Städel Museum in Frankfurt am Main.

THE GOSPEL OF THE EARLY CHRISTIAN COMMUNITY 117

THE GOSPEL OF THE EARLY CHRISTIAN COMMUNITY

Above: The napkin of Michael Wolgemut, the teacher of Albrecht Dürer (ca. 1450), in the Church of Saint Lawrence in Nürnberg.

Left: Vera Icon. The Holy Face of Christ. Westphalen (ca. 1400). From the gallery of paintings in the Kulturforum in Berlin.

One of those from whom men hide their faces,
    spurned, and we held him in no esteem.

Yet it was our infirmities that he bore,
    our sufferings that he endured,
While we thought of him as stricken,
    as one smitten by God and afflicted.

But he was pierced for our offenses,
    crushed for our sins....

Though he was harshly treated, he submitted
    and opened not his mouth;
Like a lamb led to the slaughter
    or a sheep before the shearers,
    he was silent and opened not his mouth.

Oppressed and condemned, he was taken away,
> and who would have thought any more
> of his destiny?
When [H]e was cut off from the land of the living....

Because of his affliction
> he shall see the light in fullness of days
> [Is 53:2–5, 7–8, 11 (NAB)]

In Manoppello, however, we too see on his face a preliminary radiance of the light that he beheld, as in the hour of his transfiguration on Tabor, a few hills further across the Sea of Gennesaret from where he had proclaimed to us the message of the Sermon on the Mount: "Blessed are the poor in spirit, for theirs is the kingdom of heaven. Blessed are those who mourn, for they shall be comforted. Blessed are the meek.... Blessed are you when men revile you and persecute you and utter all kinds of evil against you falsely on my account. Rejoice and be glad, for your reward is great in heaven.... You are the salt of the earth.... You are the light of the world" [Mt 5:3–5, 11–14].

Both cloths hold images of light, the one faint and shadowy, the other extremely clear. The one burial cloth is gigantic; in the other napkin, his portrait is exactly the size of a human head, in which we perceive him alive, yet after his death and not before—with the wounds of his Passion, yet freed, tranquil, benevolent. The shroud in Turin contains, besides the delicate image, many other bloodstains of the tortured man also; the napkin

The sudarium of Christ. Detail of a fresco by Benozzo Gozzoli (ca. 1450) in the choir of the Church of Saints Dominic and Sixtus in Rome.

121

shows the slain "Lamb of God" intact and thoroughly pure and cleansed, with a "face that closely unites pain and sorrow and light as only love can", as Archbishop Bruno Forte told me in 2004 when he had just become acquainted with the veil.

Here he is, the one who walks through locked doors and shows his disciples the wounds of the nails in his wrists and feet and the wound of the lance in his side. Here he is, the one who breathes on the disciples and says, "Receive the Holy Spirit" [Jn 20:22]. The one who says, "Handle me, and see" [Lk 24:39]. Or "Children, have you anything here to eat?" [cf. Jn 21:5, Lk 24:41]. Here he is, the one who sends them into the whole world and explains Scripture on the way to Emmaus and wishes them peace and breaks bread with them. When he says to them, "I am with you always, to the close of the age" [Mt 28:20], and the apostles whisper to one another, "It is the Lord!" when the Risen One comes to meet them [Jn 21:7]—so he is here also. Or when they, like Thomas, fall to their knees with the words, "My Lord and my God!" [Jn 20:28]—so he is here also. Indeed, every word of the Sermon on the Mount is stored up in this face, and the incomprehensible mercy of God, without the slightest hint of revenge. *Deus Caritas est!* God is love. Here it looks at us.

Together the two cloths depict that "mystery of faith" that Catholics to this day praise again and again, ever anew, after the transformation of bread and wine into the Body and Blood of Christ, with the words, "We proclaim your Death, O Lord, and profess your Resurrection until you come again." Yes, in these two cloths the mystery of the Christian faith is presented as in no other document. They marvelously fill up the brief text of the Gospel. They are both without parallel in the great multimedia library of our history, which indeed is overflowing with depictions of the Crucified One and with portraits of the face of Christ. The two together are the implicit reference point of all those paintings, being the TRUE IMAGE. If you tried to scan all the icons of the early Church and all the images of Christ from the first half of the second millennium into a computer and calculate their average, then this twofold image matrix would appear among them as the essence of the images of Christ and as the original standard of all our pictures of Jesus of Nazareth. Together they dispel as though with the wave of a hand the claim that we do not know what awaits us after death. For we do know WHO awaits us. Christians alone know this. Only Christians recognize God's face.

For this reason, finally, the double image also solves the riddle of why there is not a single word in all four Gospels about what Jesus looked like. This was certainly not because the face in which God had showed his features was somehow insignificant. Quite the contrary. It was because this face was described right at the beginning, in this Gospel of the early Christian community, by two images more precisely than any words ever could have done. Accordingly, none of the Evangelists needed to waste words on his face, his expression, his height, his hairstyle or his build. A pictorial miracle enlightened us from the very beginning concerning the beautiful face of God, in a laboratory of the dear Lord himself, in the tomb of Christ, which he transformed into the chamber at the heart of Christian revelation.

Vera Icon in a stained glass window of Bohemian origin (ca. 1400), in the Church of Saint Martha, Nürnberg.

THE REVOLUTION OF IMAGES

The oldest Marian icon in Rome on the screen of a smartphone, the latest product of communications technology in December 2009.

THE REVOLUTION OF IMAGES

"Did you say that?" I asked Ellen. "Did you say that the devotees of the Shroud of Turin will become a Christian sect if they do not open their minds sometime in the future and accept the napkin too, and vice versa?" She was at the steering wheel and looked over at me. "No, I just asked you about G. K. Chesterton and how he defined heresies." Now I remembered. Heresies, the witty genius of the early twentieth century had recognized, were partial truths gone wild. They are partial truths that mistook themselves for the whole truth and therefore repeatedly produced horrible errors. Viewed in this way, it really is not immaterial if we consider one or the other half of what was left in Christ's tomb as the whole estate.

"Are you talking to yourself again?" my wife asked.

"No," I laughed, "but I probably should conclude the book about the Shroud of Turin with a speech in defense of the whole package, if we are now to have a broader overview of it at last."

"Excuse me?"

"I'm asking you. Shouldn't I say that in studying the history of the Shroud, it only makes sense, basically, to speak about the two burial cloths together? Because, after all, at the beginning they were mentioned together, and now suddenly both of them start to tell, in a completely new way, about the Incarnation and Resurrection of the Son of God! Didn't you once say that the two, taken together, speak about the true meaning of the Passion

The road from Rome to the East runs behind Avezzano through the man-made plain of Fucino on the site of what was until the nineteenth century the largest inland lake in Italy.

and about the fact that we ourselves do not have to fear torture and death? Precisely now, when the churches are emptying out as never before! Precisely now, in the new age of images! Now, didn't you say that?"

"But that is what we have been saying the whole time. I never know which of us first said what—when we're not arguing, that is, but actually not even then. But I had also asked you earlier what you want to write about the fact that the shroud came to light again with the discovery of analog photography, whereas the napkin was found again almost exactly one hundred years later with the invention of digital photography." What was I supposed to say about that? It was really striking, but I didn't know what to think. Besides speculations, one could hardly say anything on that subject.

Analog and digital photography have contributed enormously to the rediscovery of the two images but at the same time have twice given rise to suggestive but misleading theories that the images too are a sort of photo, one negative and one positive—just because they involve perplexing phenomena that we know otherwise only from photos. Nevertheless, it is jumping to a completely wrong conclusion to identify them with photographs of any sort whatsoever. To be photos, both cloths would have had to lie as taut and flat over the body and face of Jesus as a piece of celluloid film stretched tight inside an old camera. But to date no one has ventured to say that. Nevertheless, many people have already gone far down that track, with fatal consequences for the proof of credibility that it was supposed to provide. Anyone who spends even five minutes attentively in front of the shroud and the napkin sees immediately that an overwhelming number of phenomena distinguish the two images from photos or daguerreotypes. Even more stirring is the neat new theory that the

Shroud of Turin may have come about through a nuclear flash that we are supposed to imagine as a sort of byproduct of the Resurrection. Yet a flash, like any lamp or source of light, radiates and dispels darkness in all directions. A flash that had not immediately burned up the cloths would have projected a mash of light onto the cloths but never an image.

But what does it matter? Being around the cloths can easily make a person giddy from the thrill of discovery and sheer childlike imagination—but also from that aggressive furor with which reckless surmises are defended against all demands of plausibility. "Now what are you thinking up?" Ellen startled me out of my musings. "Tell me about it instead. And I will tell you right away and again if I cannot see what you are saying, and then you can just forget about it." She was right, and unfortunately it was not very encouraging. An enormous confusion has taken hold of this momentous topic. It seems almost impossible to free the images from this thicket. It is as though someone has put a hex on it. That is why I had actually not wanted to set out on this long journey at all. Neither had I wanted to write this book anymore: I would have much preferred a new cookbook (and now my mouth is watering too). I did not want any more grief—and yet I was then caught by an assignment from my publisher that I could not sidestep.

And now because of it we were on the road again; we had just passed the village of

Veiled hands while touching holy relics: the crown of thorns in Paris and the mandylion in Constantinople.

Next spread: The stained glass pictorial miracle of the Sainte Chapelle (1244–1248).

The Revolution of Images

Cese and the city of Avezzano and were driving along the northern edge of the Piana del Fucino, on the old road that formerly skirted what used to be the largest inland lake in Italy, which Promethean engineering skills had transformed into a fruitful plain in the nineteenth century. Silvery fog lay over the high-altitude valley, as though the soul of the old lake were unwilling to leave the place to this day. To the left, autumn dipped the mountains of the Abruzzi in golden light. I had no idea what else I should write. All the clever thoughts that I had been pushing ahead of myself for a long time now like moraines [deposits in front of a glacier] seemed to have grown shallow. I no longer wanted to go into all the books that repeated so many false arguments with tiresome monotony. I did not want to let myself be provoked again by the shrugs or raised eyebrows of a professor to write a polemical work, so as to explain to them once more and in vain that the burial cloths are more than pious folklore. And why should I? I love pious folklore. I didn't want to argue anymore—and far and wide I saw no one who could somehow prove to me conclusively that the shroud and the napkin, these two cloths, are not plainly and simply identical with the cloths to which the Evangelist John so clearly refers in his Gospel of the Resurrection.

I have already explained that there were good reasons why John could not mention the images inscribed on the cloths. He simply could not, unless he wanted to put their very existence in extreme danger. But I no longer wanted to set right all the many hasty and premature conclusions of so many venerable scholars—errors in their research into the Shroud of Turin and its path through history that had accumulated into a veritable mountain. What else should they have done but attribute all references to a mysterious original

image exclusively to the one large cloth—as long as the little napkin was simply not there to inspect? Since I first reported five years previously on its rediscovery, developments in our world of everyday experience have arrived in increasingly rapid succession, concluding with a revolution in our pants pocket. All earlier developments suddenly pale before the development of the iPhone, even more than the recent acquisition of e-mail eclipsed fax machines, which were not much older. Now

THE REVOLUTION OF IMAGES

Explosion of visual stimuli in the Ginza district in Tokyo—the final prelude before the invasion of images in the digital revolution.

in almost any place in Europe I could download encyclical of the pope on "love in truth" (a text with 213,000 characters) into a handheld apparatus, or YouTube performances by anyone, all for the same inexpensive flat rate. What can we expect next?

Things are going to continue explosively along these lines. Should I deal with theoretical constructs of the past century in which one fantasy chases the next? Should I present such houses of cards once again before knocking them down? The nuclear flash theory, the dogma of the "*sindon* folded four times", the tissue of extremely dubious identifications, the Veronica theory or other touching legends? For indeed, one thing remains in all these developmental leaps of ever-more-fleeting communications technologies, and that is the images themselves. The images remain. They are not only lasting and stable—their significance increases constantly, and this paves the way at a frantic pace for a development that, as we can expect, will conclude in a quantum leap of consciousness no less momentous than the fall of the Berlin Wall. That will be the definitive recognition of the image as the ultimate storage medium, as a pictorial document and an extremely complex conveyance of data, which does not have to take second place behind any supertext. Quite the contrary. It is a revolution of images, such as people of the Middle Ages perhaps once experienced when they came out of their dingy huts and houses and for the first time set foot in the gleaming architectural marvel of the Sainte Chapelle, which suddenly told them about God's action in history in radiant stained glass. That too was a revolution. The billboards and flickering advertising towers from Shanghai to Tokyo are, at any rate, only a faint foretaste of what still awaits us.

"Can't you dial that back and say it more simply," Ellen said, "or are your readers supposed to close the book for good at that point because they won't settle for anything less than the red carpet treatment?" For heaven's sake, no, I laughed, and promised to tell instead the instructive tale about the sad fate of the FAZ magazine for which I worked until ten years ago. This was the full-color insert that accompanied the Friday edition of the *Frankfurter Allgemeine Zeitung*. That was why every Friday in the editing department of the newspaper—where many referred to our magazine only as "*die Bunte*"—some of our venerable colleagues had the knack of shaking the magazine out of the paper and into the wastebasket without even touching it. They didn't even want to

handle *that*. Pictures! In color! How primitive! Afterward, they turned sensuously again to the "newsprint" of the paper, the pages full of little letters; the only regret that many had was that they were unfortunately no longer produced by lead type. *Sola scriptura!* Only script and nothing but script alone! I don't need to explain that any further here. These were the last offshoots of the age of Gutenberg, which was now being flooded by a tsunami of new images, in the iPhones, on YouTube, on every television screen. Shouldn't we then understand the mere existence of these images on the cloths from the tomb in a new way today as a unique quantum leap in the history of religion? And aren't we obliged ultimately to take these pictorial documents as seriously, as "texts", as the Egyptians did with their hieroglyphics and as our computers do quite self-evidently by way of a simple binary code? After all, it can no longer be too early to start. For indeed, these are not just any images. It is instead the image of God.

"Ecco la generazione, o Signore, che cerca il tuo volto, Dio di Giacobbe!" we heard this morning in the Convent of the Rosary on the Monte Mario in Rome, before we set out on our journey. This is a verse from Psalm 24: "Such is the generation of those who seek him, who seek the face of the God of Jacob" [v. 6]. That may have been the deepest longing of ancient Israel: to see at last the face of God, who had led his people out of slavery. Already the Book of Genesis, the first book of the Jewish Bible, spoke about man being made in the image of God, right at the beginning. Yet Christians first had the privilege of experiencing how much God finally made himself like us. Right afterward, they began to paint icons, at first of the Mother of God. For indeed, God himself had already made an icon of her Son. The apostles were the first human beings to see before them again in the napkin the One who would be waiting for them too after their martyrdom. Since then, the image of God has been for all the baptized the bridge over the abyss of death. You have only to look him in the eyes in order to avoid falling. He gives us wings. God surely waits for every human being, but we know him. We recognize his face. "Lord, now lettest thou thy servant depart in peace, according to thy word; for mine eyes have seen thy salvation which thou hast prepared in the presence of all peoples", the aged seer Simeon exclaimed in the Temple in Jerusalem when he saw the newborn Jesus on Mary's arm [Lk 2:29–32]. The infant had not said a word to him, much less given a Sermon on the Mount or even just told a clever parable. Perhaps he did not even look at the seer but was sleeping. Yet Simeon had seen in his features the face of God, in the countenance of a helpless baby. Since then, we are all allowed, with Simeon, to depart in peace.

We have the images, but unfortunately we don't show them. Christendom has the image of God. But it doesn't show it. It is grotesque—inconceivable, actually. For can Christians do anything less than tell about the image of God that they have? "I think", I said to my wife, "that until now something has gone completely wrong in recounting this unique story of the Millennium: of this re-entry of the True Icon of God's human face in history, of this simply incredible rediscovery. Somehow people can't get it through their heads. Therefore, I think that now the time has finally come to simplify the story of the burial cloths radically. And to do that, I think, we may have to detach ourselves from history altogether and tell the story over again in a radically phenomenological way."

"That doesn't sound simpler."

"Oh, but it is. What I mean is this: we must stick much more closely to visual perception—in other words, what the cloths show today and what old documents or texts show us about them. If old pictures show us the face of Christ with the eyes open, we can no longer simply identify the image, willy-nilly, with the Shroud of Turin, however well it may fit in with our theory. If it shows a little lock of hair at the forehead, we must quite simply identify it with the napkin, where that lock of hair can be seen clearly. Above all, though, we must admit that we basically have only two essential reference points. The one is our observation of the cloths today, and the other is the first mention of the cloths around two thousand years ago by John. The greater part of the history in between we can simply forget, until the moment when they both come to light. For the shroud, that is the year 1356, when it was first displayed in Lirey, and for the napkin, it is the first public exhibition by Pope Innocent II in Rome in 1208. Of course, both cloths already existed before that, because they simply cannot be medieval creations. Nevertheless, all other hypotheses and attributions are, in their details, almost always speculations—and now and then simply false, whether well intentioned or not, whether knowingly or unwittingly."

"Excuse me? You want to bracket off the whole first millennium from now on? Surely you can't be serious."

"But I am. No, not the whole millennium … Or maybe I do. Of course, the cloths existed in the meantime also. Personally, I have good reasons to be convinced that most of the testimonies—from Edessa to Constantinople—refer to the little napkin and not to the large shroud. I don't want to repeat all the passages, but it seems unambiguous to me that the image with the face is almost always meant. The first clear representation of the double figure on the shroud, at any rate, is found on a pilgrim's plaque from Lirey from the year 1356. It is also instructive that the napkin was displayed much earlier than the large Shroud."

"How so?"

"First of all, technically. The little cloth was of course always much easier to display than the four-meter-long panel of material. Any bishop could easily show the napkin to the faithful with two hands, or any commander to his soldiers. Above all, though, even the Jews in Edessa no longer could tell from the image on the napkin its origins in the unclean tomb—as opposed to the shroud with the many bloodstains of the Crucified One. It was therefore much easier to break the spell for the napkin. That is why it could be released much earlier from the *arcanum* of early Christianity, because the spotless image was no longer reminiscent of death and dying or a tomb at all. Everything that we can read about the rediscovery of the legendary *mandylion* in a city gate of Edessa in 544 therefore points particularly to the napkin that is now in Manoppello but not to the shroud, as almost all sindonologists have long maintained."

"You're sure?"

"At least as sure as the contrary statement, but really even more certain. I can't prove it now—but it is clear that all statements detailing the whereabouts of the cloths from the tomb until Lirey and Rome are pure assumptions, speculations and conjectures. The only sure thing is that the cloths had already existed for ages before their arrival in the West. They are not medieval creations, and there is no way that they could be creations of the Byzantine or Carolingian world of images. I suspect that for a long time they were simply preserved together—first in Jerusalem, then in Edessa, and finally in Constantinople, and that they brought along with them the aura of mystery and secrecy, which was taken for granted

for several centuries. That cannot be proved. Written testimonies concerning the cloths from Byzantium and the East are always ambiguous. Even the key document of all shroud aficionados, the formal speech of a certain Archdeacon Gregory on the occasion of the delivery of the *sindon* to Emperor Romanus I in the year 944, is extremely ambiguous. A miniature found in the eleventh-century Codex Skylitzes, which shows that same scene, could very well be depicting both cloths at the same time. Or else a scene in which the image of Christ's countenance not made by human hands is presented to the emperor for veneration by a deacon whose hands are veiled in the same way in which priests and deacons would hand over a chalice containing the Body and Blood of Christ in the liturgy. Or like the veiled hands of the angels in the Sainte Chapelle in Paris, which hold aloft the sacred crown of thorns to be venerated.

"The first unambiguous description of the large *sindon* is a report of the Crusader Robert de Clary from the fateful year 1204, in which he speaks about the cloth 'in which the Lord was wrapped' being on display in Constantinople completely unfolded. Generally, though, they are all obscure texts that talk about a bright image. Of course, the names are often mixed up, so that to this day we cannot tell exactly which of the two cloths was actually meant when the *sindon*, the *soudarion*, the *mandylion*, the picture of Edessa, the picture of Abgar, the imprinted image or the 'four-fold' was mentioned. Since antiquity, the cloths in Oviedo or Cahors have also been called "sweat cloths", that is, *sudarium* in Spain and *suaire* in France. Only now—with the help of the rediscovered napkin in Manoppello—does the fog clear somewhat. During this period of a gradually brightening obscurity, therefore, it is rarely (if ever) easy to tell which of the two cloths is

King Abgar receives the image of Christ from the hands of the apostle Jude Thaddeus (painting by Franz Ludwig Hermann [1733], Monastery church in Lindau).

the subject of a given source—and I have long since stopped believing anyone who says that he knows precisely which."

"But explain one thing to me: why you are so obsessed with the 'four-fold' cloth?"

"I'm not obsessed with it. *Tetradiplon* is just an old Greek name—no, more precisely, an old clear characterization of the cloth that has misled researchers of the past century to develop an extremely subtle and complicated theory of how we are supposed to imagine that the Shroud of Turin was folded in the early centuries and had to be stored in a box so that at last it corresponded exactly to that term. A highly complex little doctrinal construct came about, with a lot of waxworks tricks from the county fairs of yore, in order to make the expression 'folded four times' apply to the shroud and to salvage it as a testimony. It was a filigreed and equally ambitious glass bead game [*Glasperlenspiel*, an allusion to Hermann Hesse's novel *Siddhartha*] with the history of tradition. Nevertheless, on the napkin in Manoppello today any observer can see with the naked eye that this little cloth has *four distinct folds*. This image fits the description *tetradiplon* like an egg in an egg cup."

"Well, is there a name that applied to both images and cloths?"

"Yes, both cloths were always designated by the Greek term *acheiropoieton*, which means 'not made by human hands'."

"So that is what we read in the documents, if I understand you correctly. But didn't you want to use a phenomenological method this time? Didn't you say that you wanted above all to let the images speak to the topic? Then what do the old copies of the images look like?"

"I already mentioned one of them earlier, dating from the eleventh century, in which a so-called *mandylion* is being handed to Emperor Romanus I in the year 944. Researchers are virtually unanimous in identifying it as the shroud. Nevertheless, I recognize it above all as the napkin. In the first millennium I simply find no image that convinces me that it is depicting the shroud but find many that portray the face on the napkin. In the treasury of Saint Peter's Basilica, the oldest cross, which Emperor Justin II sent to Rome from Byzantium around the year 570, displays two medallions with the face of Christ, for which the napkin was probably the model: the open eyes, the hair, even the tiny little lock of hair on the forehead. Then too, many frescoes and icons in Eastern Orthodoxy speak to this very day again and again about the napkin in particular. As to veneration, therefore, the *Sanctum Sudarium* has precedence over the Holy shroud. And remarkably, that is true once again for Western Christendom, where the *sudarium* came to Rome earlier and was exhibited publicly at a considerably earlier date. That is why, in East and West, there were also a great many icons and images inspired by the image of Christ on the napkin—long before the first copy of the complete shroud existed. Instead, the shroud, well into the High Middle Ages, served as the center of secret ceremonies and liturgies—for instance, in the military order of the Knights Templar, which probably took possession of it in 1204 during the Fourth Crusade in the chaos of the capture of Constantinople and brought it to the West."

"And what does that mean today?"

"It means that we should consider ourselves fortunate. The napkin resolves many contradictions that the Shroud of Turin posed until now. Two images make the coordination of many old documents much easier; for often it is like scales falling from your eyes. But merely saying that precipitates an academic dispute into which I would rather not be drawn."

"Why not? What is the problem, if the arguments are valid?"

"Well, first of all, there's the human factor: the usual jealousy and other understandable sensitivities. The fear that one may have made oneself ridiculous by an error. That is stupid, but that's how it is. Comparable cases are well known in almost all academic disciplines. And then the research community devoted to the *Santa Sindone* moves these days like a huge tanker that really should change course now after the reappearance of the napkin. But of course, that doesn't happen so quickly. Hence, leading sindonologists until now continue to ignore the little *sudarium* or try to ridicule it. For history does not need to be rewritten as a result of its reappearance, but some books do. Naturally, not everyone finds that pleasant."

"Is that just a feeling that you have, or do you have some concrete evidence to prove it?"

"Well, ever since Pope Benedict XVI visited Manoppello on September 1, 2006, no one can say anymore that the napkin is still unknown. Nevertheless, in Turin the napkin has not been duly noted, to put it mildly. The objection goes: It has not yet been studied sufficiently. Therefore, it would have to be examined scientifically for decades so as to prove what a blind man can tell by feeling it."

"But you don't really mean to claim that you are going to explain something that has remained hidden to science until now, do you?"

"Reluctantly. Actually, I would prefer not to. But someone has to do it. For it has remained hidden not just to science but to the whole world—and to the greater part of Christendom, in which the news about a true image of God had survived only as a rumor."

"Well, hello! Do you want to argue with the whole world now and not just with me, for a change? Don't you think that that sounds utterly insane?" From the beginning, my wife had liked even less than I did the fact that I had accepted the assignment for this book, and I could understand her perspective. It is probably not fun for any woman to have an old "pregnant" man beside her for months.

"Don't worry", I tried to reassure her for the hundredth time. "You can't blame anyone for it. Many errors were, as I said, almost compulsory. Because the napkin with the face of Christ, after its disappearance from Rome, vanished from the sight of Christendom for over four hundred years, gradually almost all testimonies from the first millennium to one or the other image were assigned to the one large burial cloth in the research of the past century. The true image with the face of Christ had simply vanished from the radar screen of Christendom like a flying object that had disappeared again into the depths of the universe. But it was also precisely the time when modern science was developing as never before. So increasingly all the historical testimonies and sources were referred during that period only to the one relic that continued to remain in view. That was the great Shroud of Turin."

A few minutes earlier we had passed the serpentine city of Cucullo, which now lay behind us to the left. Now Ellen steered the car toward Italy's Valle Reale, where the rugged Abruzzi mountains open to the lovely landscape of the Adriatic hills. I looked to the right, past Sulmona and up the mountain slope, where the ruins of Pietro Morrone's hermitage are concealed; he was the holy hermit who suffered a complete shipwreck when he was elected pope in 1294 against his will, took the name Celestine V, rode into L'Aquila on a donkey and shortly thereafter threw in the towel and resigned himself to spending his twilight years incarcerated behind grilles. The "angelic pope", as he was called by his adherents, would have been familiar already with Christ's *sudarium* but certainly not with the shroud. Generations and generations did not have what we have today: both cloths, both images—the true image!—although they perhaps had a more or less unshakable belief that they existed.

"And what is it all supposed to mean?" our oldest son, Raam, asked us last summer in Wangen, in the beautiful Allgäu region [in Swabia], above the roofs of the old city, when we visited him in Germany and told him a little about all this.

"What is it supposed to mean? They ought to help us and remind us that God is Person", said Ellen, even before I could answer. "That therefore no people, no doctrinal construct, no shrine is at the center of our faith but rather a personal encounter with Christ. That God was visible among us and will remain visible forever."

"Try a little experiment", I added. "We both know by now a whole series of people who are no longer alive. What do you think of first when you remember them? Their deeds, their words—the good as well as the bad? Their masterpieces or their failures? No, I don't think so. It is always their faces that first come to mind. Persons are always depicted first and foremost by their faces, in life and in memory. The image of God answers questions about death and eternal life."

"Well," said our oldest son, "we all have to die. But how does that affect our life on earth today, before death? Or the renewal of the world? Or a just reorganization of society? Or the reform of Christianity, which is always necessary?" His wife Ruth had just given birth to their third daughter, Priscilla, who listened to our conversation in her cradle with her eyes closed, preoccupied with the difficulties of digestion as well as with getting used to the world, the light of which she had first glimpsed only one month before. Of course, her father's questions were more than justified, even in wealthy Germany, near Lake Constance, above the city wall of the peaceful city of Wangen.

"The cloths are storage media, on which the Passion and Resurrection of Christ are encoded", I started elusively, trying not to become too enthusiastic, unfortunately in vain. "Much of it will not be legible until tomorrow or the day after tomorrow. The cloths are umpteen times more complex and sophisticated than the message that NASA launched into deep space as news about mankind. For heaven's sake, therefore, we cannot think too little of them. These are, after all, the most precious images in the world, no less precious than the entire Sistine Chapel! And then there is something else that is immensely important, especially today, in our superficial advertising- and media-driven society. I mean the so-called branding, which is important for every society, for every firm and likewise for every product. A good trademark is worth more than its weight in gold or platinum. Take for example the Coca-Cola bottle or the Mercedes star! But nothing in this world surpasses identification with a face. If Christianity were a company the face of God would be its unique "selling

point". You could say a lot more about this. Indeed, that is one advantage of the papacy too. In Benedict XVI the Catholic Church has a face—just as formerly she had one in the face of John Paul II, and so on and so forth. How much more of an advantage, though, there is in the face of Christ himself. Rediscovering his face is more important for Christ's Church than the discovery of the theory of relativity or the discovery of America."

Our firstborn son, who had known me long enough, continued to look skeptically at me. Probably, quite certainly, he too saw that I really didn't know everything that I was saying and what it was all supposed to mean. So finally I said that to him also: "I do not know. I don't know what it is all supposed to mean. My heart catches fire when I look at these images, every time, more and more, and it consoles me. That much I know."

"But do we need these cloths in order to believe? Do Ruth and I need them? Do our daughters need these images? Did all the martyrs and saints need these cloths, or all the brave missionaries who traveled everywhere, from Africa to China, risking their hides for the Gospel? Do we need them in order to have faith?"

"Thank you", I said, in unison with Ellen. "That is the point. After all, it is not a question of whether we need the two cloths. It is a gift to help us believe. Already it seems as though the appearance of these images has caused a sigh of relief to be heard through many monasteries, throughout the Church, throughout the world. It is therefore much rather like Christmas, when an especially large package is lying under the Christmas tree, this time with the inscription: 'From God personally, with love.' Do we then ask whether we need it? Are we not then simply curious and extremely grateful? It is an unopened letter of heaven to earth. For after all, this is the *sindon* and this is the *soudarion* from Christ's tomb, and nothing else. They exist, these cloths from the chamber of Christ's Resurrection, which Peter and John found in his empty tomb on the first Easter morning. We have them here. Besides the Eucharist and Sacred Scripture, these cloths are among the greatest gifts to Christendom—especially in our time. Whether or not we need them is therefore not quite the right question. I told you already that I do not know what it is all supposed to mean; nor am I acquainted with anyone who knows. Only one thing do I know: precisely for our time, the two cloths are one unique gift. Thank God."

With the eyes of the seer Simeon, the Wisdom of Israel recognizes the human face of God (painting by Rembrandt von Rijn, National Museum, Stockholm).

THE STONE
THAT WAS
ROLLED AWAY

*The little town of Manoppello at the
foot of the Majella massif in the Abruzzi
region, along the old Via Tiburtina
from Rome to Pescara.*

Whenever the Shroud of Turin is brought out of the darkness of its vault for a few weeks, millions come to see the sensation. The napkin, in contrast, is hidden in plain daylight. Yet that is precisely what makes it especially difficult for many people to accept the fact that it is just as authentic as the shroud. For the *sudarium* is hiding in public, so to speak. It is concealed in a place with incredibly free access. All this makes it implausible. The *Santa Sindone*, as we said, was exhibited only four times in the last century. There is no fixed rhythm to it. How much easier would it be, though, to understand the value of the napkin if it were as well concealed and inaccessible as it used to be here in Manoppello or in Rome, in Byzantium, in Edessa, when it was shown briefly in a procession once a year and then locked away again? Or if it were to disappear for decades at a time in a vault like the Shroud of Turin? Then it would be much easier to consider this extremely fine fabric as the crown jewel of Christendom. And then millions would stream to the exhibitions in the Abruzzi region as they hurried in early 2010 to Turin. (And in Manoppello they might find only a few rooms, hardly enough for a large pilgrimage.)

The fact that the *Sanctum Sudarium* has been instead so easily accessible for several years, however, in the simplest possible illumination, understandably makes it more difficult to have confidence in its value. Here there is no crackling sea of candles. Here the idea of a "sound and light" show has not yet occurred to anyone. Thank God. Here, then, what for so long was the most precious treasure of the popes is hidden in real poverty, with a handful of Capuchin friars. God's plans are different from what we think. He slips in beneath our expectations. He surpasses our sense of humor. That is why he conceals his Son's *sudarium*

right in our midst. He does not have to have someone prove to him that it is authentic or corroborate it in a laboratory or in dubious experiments by self-styled experts in odd testing protocols. To all those who think that authenticity could not possibly be established apart from science, he whistles a tune and whispers once again a verse from Psalm 2 into their ears: "He who sits in the heavens laughs" [Ps 2:4]. That is why he has entrusted his dearest image to the simple and not to the wise.

That is why we too, at the conclusion of this journey, wanted to conceal the *sudarium* again as before—at least virtually in this book—so as to allow its secret to shine forth more brightly again. For that reason we wanted to look at it again all alone, without a stranger alongside, like Jude Thaddeus on his way to Edessa, like Mary in her last cave—like the apostles in the burial chamber behind the heavy stone that had closed it off but was now rolled back.

We had set out from Rome at around six, and now it was still early, around eight o'clock on Monday morning after Mass. You can scarcely find a human being here then. We had drunk a cup of coffee in the nearby bar, had brought two chairs up to the little marble platform behind the tabernacle in front of the napkin, prayed the Glorious Mysteries of the Rosary and were totally alone in the shrine. Once again it was sheer luck—in a window of time that cannot remain open like that for very long. No, it will not be possible much longer to enjoy this luxury of being able to spend so much time so intimately with this treasure. Yet until now pilgrims here all year round can study it up close, which was never possible in Turin. There was only one tomb, one Passion of Jesus and one Resurrection of Christ from the dead, but there were two cloths that first told about it, and here is the first of the two.

Detail of a map of the Abruzzi region by Egnazio Danti (1536–1586) in the Galleria delle carte geografiche in the Vatican Museum.

This is the clean cloth of the Resurrection after the blood-soaked cloth of suffering. It is the "cloth of cloths", as Goethe also called it, as opposed to the "book of books", which is how the Muslims revere their Qur'an. "But there are also many other things which Jesus did", John wrote at the conclusion of his Gospel. "Were every one of them to be written, I suppose that the world itself could not contain the books that would be written" [Jn 21:25]. But now obviously the time has come

when the icons that God himself wrote should begin to speak once again about what could not yet be said openly back then. Of course, that does not mean that it should be believed without further ado. Quite the contrary. The whole medium of this simple church and its primitive illumination says: It cannot be!

It is something that we experience again here each time anew. "Sit down", said Ellen, because I had stood up again, leaned my head on the pane of glass and shot what was probably my ten thousandth photo of the cloth. "In a moment!" I said, because I had again just discovered something new, an angle not yet captured, a nuance never before seen, something new and unheard of in this incredible face—which was so terrifically antithetical to the depiction of it in Turin. Almost everything about the two cloths is contrast and complementarity, in a remarkable reversal. For in contrast to the cloth locked away in Turin, this hidden cloth in the Abruzzi hills is totally unconfined. In Turin the shroud lies buried deep in a safe. The no-less-precious napkin is almost unprotected here—although in 1506 the first pillar of the new Saint Peter's Basilica was set up as the strongest vault in the world precisely for this little cloth, in the mightiest temple in Christendom. The one cloth is world famous, the other still almost unknown. The large linen cloth may weigh several kilos [more than four pounds]. The napkin made of sea silk probably weighs less than a gram, truly next to nothing. The one image shows the whole body of Jesus, the other only his countenance, with the same wounds as in Turin. Yet here they are healed, one and all. The body in Turin is depicted from the front and the back; the countenance in Manoppello can be seen from both sides. The countenance of Turin is silent; the face on the napkin is extremely expressive. The Shroud of Turin is as opaque and impenetrable as death. With the *sudarium*, an endless number of transparent shadings, lively reflections and constantly changing illuminations are part of the nature and essence of the image. There is no "objective photo" of it, because there is no objectively valid general look of it.

Perhaps the "colors" of the two images are nevertheless similar and only the materials fundamentally different because—aside from the blood on the shroud—there are no pigments on them. Therefore, some have tried to imagine the fascinating coloration of the napkin as similar to the blue in the feathers of a kingfisher, which is evoked on our retinas not by pigments embedded in them but rather by a structure within the feathers that refracts and disperses sunlight in such a way that it is sometimes reflected as sapphire blue and sometimes as emerald green. Yet that too is a conceptual model devised to approximate the inexplicable phenomenon of this image. On January 25, 2007, I was present when a camera team from ZDF [Zweites Deutsches Fernsehen, or Second German television] recently declared a red glimmer on one temple of the portrait as the discovery of a particle of pigment. Yet all you had to do was change the viewing angle a bit, and there was no red glimmer or any other color at that same spot. On April 30, 2007, Professor Pietro Baraldi from Modena examined the fabric once again, millimeter by millimeter, with a Raman microscope and determined that no pigments of any sort can be found on the veil. Polish researchers from Danzig have found that the fibers of the sea silk can serve as a storage medium for light, as we might imagine that other sorts of information are stored in the silicon of the microchips in our computers. Yet no one to date has been able to give a plausible explanation for the origin and the presence of the image on the veil. The same is true of the large burial cloth in Turin. Both are "photo-graphs", "images of light" in the etymological and original sense of the word. Both are extremely faint and seem to float in the fibers of the different textiles,

The former Church of Saint Michael on Tarigni Hill behind Manoppello. In the background is the Gran Sasso, the highest mountain in Italy.

THE STONE THAT WAS ROLLED AWAY

especially again right now, in the morning light of the shrine. If necessary, then I will gladly and briefly repeat for the hundredth time that no other woven artifact is the napkin that John writes about except this little cloth that was shimmering opposite me again, just twenty centimeters [eight inches] away from my eyes.

And then even I tell myself again right away: But this cannot be true at all! This little veil cannot simply be the "true image" of Christ, which once drew more pilgrims to Rome than to Santiago de Compostela. There were millions of them, even centuries before the later streams of pilgrims to Turin! You may simply not buy the idea that this Capuchin church with its neon lights should be concealing that same missing treasure. That this little cloth in front of us is supposed to be the first

Still undisturbed. The centuries-long sleep of the beautiful Vera Icon is coming to an end only now in our days.

page of the Gospels, which records the first news of Christ's Resurrection. The thought just does not compute. Our gray cells rebel against it as they do against the assumption that this little cloth, together with the Shroud of Turin, passed through the hands of Peter and the other apostles. And through the hands of Mary, his Mother, and later through the hands of emperors and popes. That exceeds the power of imagination. It does not compute. Basically, the thing to be believed here is a trifle, but somehow you just can't do it—although Christians for two thousand years have sworn that they were convinced of the Resurrection of Christ from the dead.

The little cloth over the tabernacle in the old Church of Saint Michael beyond the little town of Manoppello in the Abruzzi hills challenges us to have precisely this faith as no theological polemic has done for centuries. It draws us out of our safety zone. It unmasks: this veil reveals a forgotten truth. The gaze of the Risen One instructs us gently and unobtrusively. It clarifies an enormous loss. Therefore, it makes it clearer than any clever analysis why so many Europeans are afraid of minarets. For many years now, even in the churches, an ever-increasing number of people scarcely know the faith that actually unites Christians and holds them together—not to mention the "faith" of atheists. The face of God, however, continues to be the polestar of Christianity, around which the universe revolves. By setting its sights on this face, Europe developed over the centuries as the most splendid continent on the globe. He is the ruler of the recurring image of the heavenly Jerusalem; he is the Lamb seated upon the throne, as the seer John wrote at the end of his life [see Rev 7:17]. Yet is this face really lost? Not at all. Here it is, in fact. We just stopped looking at it. The polestar does not move from the spot. We always

Six o'clock in the morning. Father Carmine Cucinelli, guardian of the Capuchin friars at the Basilica of the Holy Face, has just opened the main entrance to ventilate the shrine.

see it exactly in the north. But nowadays, isn't all that just unbelievable? Of course it is. Now the two cloths are no longer threatened by laws of ritual purity, as they were in the beginning, but instead are threatened by a no-less-powerful taboo of the modern era: ridiculousness. That is probably why, in a mysterious way, now the successor of the apostle Peter is again involved with recovering the true and most important image in the world, just like

Peter at the beginning, in the tomb, in the light of the dawn of Christianity on the first Easter morning, in the midst of the confusion of the digital revolution, which links and entangles the truth with all sorts of insanity.

Six days after the present successor of Peter had visited and contemplated the old *sudarium*—the first pope to do so in five hundred years—Benedict XVI exclaimed in Saint Peter's Square [in his general audience] on

September 6, 2006, that "we can certainly say that God gave himself a human face, the Face of Jesus, and consequently, from now on, if we truly want to know the Face of God, all we have to do is to contemplate the Face of Jesus! In his Face we truly see who God is and what he looks like!" Three years later he said to his former students in Castel Gandolfo: "We do not grope in the dark, we do not wander in vain seeking what might be righteous, we are not like sheep without a shepherd who do not know which is the right path. God has manifested himself." That was a few weeks ago, on August 30, 2009, when he announced that in nine months he intended to travel to Turin as a pilgrim on May 2, 2010, and also asked, "What kind of Catholic would not want to rejoice, so to speak, or be proud of the fact that God has shown himself to us, has shown us his Face, and that his wisdom assumes its definitive form in the Crucified, as opposed to the folly that mistakes itself for wisdom?" Shouldn't this joy, however, rise up again in us? He went on to ask: "Should we not be glad that in the confusion of the world, in the hopelessness of philosophy and of religious theories and opinions, we are privileged to see the Face of God in Christ?"

Light from light. The midday sun of the Adriatic is reflected in a side window of the shrine of the human face of God among us.

THE
DIVINE
KALEIDOSCOPE

*The sudarium of Christ over the high altar
of the Basilica of the Holy Face, with the
rose window over the main entrance shining
through and reflections from the apse.*

Bruno Forte, the bishop of nearby Chieti, might have said the same; he had invited the pope then to Manoppello and later remarked that the countenance on the Holy Veil could be understood precisely as a pictorial translation of the expression *ponim*, the Hebrew word for face. This expression, he noted, has existed since the days of early Judaism but only in the plural form: faces. And that is really true: the Holy Face in Manoppello consists of infinitely many faces, in countless reflections, with one identity: that of the divine Son of man. Confronted with

The sudarium at rest. A residue of light makes just a residue of the true image on the veil perceptible.

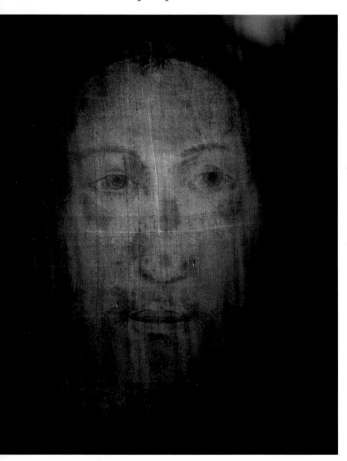

this image, therefore, a photographer could go crazy—and if I am not mistaken, many people have long since considered me mad, including some of the good Capuchin friars of Manoppello, when they see that there is no end to my photographing here. First, because the images that I see are never captured by the camera. Second, because I always see new images here. There are not enough hours in the day for me to spend in front of it. It is a divine kaleidoscope that causes the same face to shine forth in a new and different way each time, in the different light of spring, summer, fall and winter, at night, in the morning, at midday and in the evening, one way in rainy weather, another when it is sunny or in candlelight. Recently—in early September of 2009—I found the view through the veil from a very special angle toward the open main entrance in the first rays of dawn gripping as never before, before and after Lauds recited by the Capuchins, from quarter after six to quarter after seven, when the first early Mass starts on the altar beneath the image. Then every day the face of Christ has its other moment when it starts to float over the cloth, in the blue equilibrium of the light between day and night. Again, I could not stop photographing these moments, with wonderful results, and yet I was helpless in the knowledge that the truth cannot be photographed.

Here, then, it is not the photographer's skill that creates the best photos but rather, if anything, sheer luck and familiarity with the image. Only the very best photographers are allowed to get near the Shroud of Turin, under exclusive contracts, simply because exhibiting the gigantic cloth is so difficult. In contrast, on some days throngs of pilgrims, armed with their handheld cameras, already gather to see the veil—but in this case even a world-class photographer has to start from scratch, and

The Vera Icon en route. Every third Sunday in May, the Holy Face is carried in procession to the Church of Saint Nicholas and returns the following day.

the quality of his camera may or may not help. With my very inexpensive camera, I have made photos here that I was not able to repeat with a better one, and this has remained true from one apparatus to the next. And so this image is a deep well full of images, or more precisely a fresh spring, and the images that I see disappear again with a tiny turn of the viewing angle faster than trout in a mountain stream.

"What do you say, then, to people who say that the image is painted?" Ellen asked, as I finally sat down again beside her, with the camera still ready to shoot. "I don't care", I said. "It didn't come about by itself. That's the first thing. It has an author. Why shouldn't it be painted? Why shouldn't the image on the Shroud of Turin be painted too? But if so, then how and where? By whom? That is the decisive question here. For what is so striking here is the sheer, incredible restraint of the artist who created it. It is just the same in Turin. Wouldn't any artist that we know about have reached more lavishly for the brushes and paint pots for this subject?"

"But isn't the face so asymmetrical that it would be chalked up as an artistic error had it been produced by any art student?"

"You said it. The positioning of the pupils too, for example, corresponds to nothing

Transfiguration of Christ. On the eve of the feast on August 6, a second, shorter procession with the veil is held.

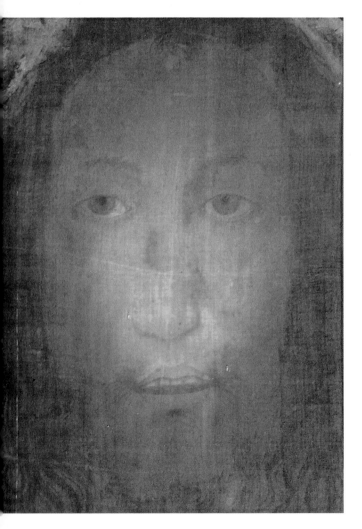

found in photographs, and the teeth aren't right, or the lock of hair at the forehead. They don't fit into the symmetry. But would we turn such observations into an objection against Picasso too? The fact that here and there he painted something crooked that he really ought to correct, if you please? This question brings us considerably closer to the essence of the cloths."

"What do you mean?"

"They are painted, but not in the manner of other painters. They are two freestyle works of art of an absolutely free artist. And so there can be some painterly riddles in Turin, or here a tooth may be crooked, and one pupil and the lock of hair, without us itching to correct the 'errors'. For we are dealing here with a greater artist than the great Picasso. Both images, however, are executed without foundation and without pigments, in a way that no human painter would ever attempt or achieve. Therefore, not only are they really not the work of Leonardo or Dürer or Picasso, and not only are they not photos, X-rays, impressions, or rubbings, or whatever else might come to mind, but they are simply two absolutely unique objects. They are two enigmatic masterpieces. They are two creations. God is not a photographer or a painter or a composer or an atomic physicist or a radiologist. He, who created heaven and earth, is nevertheless an artist—and a creative one. The image is his work. This true image was painted by the Master of all masters."

Father Carmine had walked up to us. He is the friendly Capuchin friar with the short white beard who opens the basilica every morning at six o'clock; in 2004 he was transferred here by the provincial of his order to serve as the new guardian and rector of the shrine. This unique image creation fell to his lot almost in the way that the baby Jesus in Nazareth once came into the hands of Joseph,

Benedict XVI with Father Carmine Cucinelli in front of the "true image" on September 1, 2006, on the first voluntary journey made by the pope in Italy.

his surprised, saintly foster father. In Sulmona, his previous assignment, no one had told him what awaited him here. Pilgrims here, whose many questions he has to answer, have set him right; next year he will probably be transferred again. "Yes," he says with a bit of melancholy and a smile, "all serious researchers who have devoted themselves thus far to the Holy Face come to a point where they say that this image is inexplicable." In recent years he has cautiously initiated many new investigations of the relic. In doing so, he has not let anyone hurry or pressure him. The Capuchins have proved their patience over the centuries. Therefore, Padre Carmine would never enter into competition with the shroud in Turin, which in the past hundred years has become the most prominent textile in academic research (with over 180,000 work hours, a figure that continues increase rapidly). A few days ago he had the

wooden frame of walnut around the veil taken out of the reliquary and examined. The experts found that the frame around the true image was glued and welded together in 1714 with isinglass [fish glue], so that the seal was dry and hard as a bone. Since then, the gossamer-thin veil between the two old panes of crystal was never exposed again to fresh air. Should he therefore have had the frame broken open now? He smiles and repeats once again: "Here everyone comes to the point where they say that this image is inexplicable."

That is why he smiles skeptically also at any attempt to prove that the veil and the Shroud of Turin can perhaps after all be accounted for someday, somehow, in terms of a hitherto-uninvestigated physical or chemical reaction. The images on the two extremely different fabrics cannot be explained with all the techniques of science. They go beyond the limit that you read about now and then in reports from Lourdes or other places of pilgrimage when once again an inexplicable healing occurs there. Therefore, they must be considered at least as marvelous as a "miraculous" healing that physicians declare to be scientifically inexplicable when they finally run out of their specialist jargon.

The mere fact that the cloths are not decomposed is already unbelievable. Both of them have survived for two thousand years. They have withstood wars, sieges, conflagrations, thefts and pillaging—and also all the attempts to denounce them as forgeries. They were not consumed by moths; they have not fallen to pieces. "Christian faith is a faith in miracles", the philosopher Robert Spaemann recently said with marvelous concision. This is the decisive guidepost for all investigations of the *sindon* and the *soudarion*. No one will find their secret except along the Via Crucis and the Via Lucis, along the Way of the Cross and the Way of Light. In Christ's tomb the two ways crossed—in and beneath these cloths. No one now should suppose anything less when standing before them. The death was thoroughly human, the Resurrection thoroughly divine. The blood on the *sindon* comes from Jesus of Nazareth; the light in the *soudarion* is a reflected splendor of the eternal light. The cloths are the work of man; the "images" on them, the work of God. Any attempt to derive them exclusively from some natural occurrence therefore necessarily leads to error. The event in which they came about was not natural. It burst the bonds of nature and death. That is why they too remain as inexplicable as life itself.

Only a radical faith in miracles, therefore, allows us to recognize—not understand—the nature of these pictorial miracles. Much, very much can be understood. But it would be demanding too much to try to understand everything. To be able to contemplate these images is already an infinite gain—to see that the cloths that lay together then in the tomb are together again today, in the light of worldwide publicity and therefore now also in this book. The true images are among us. We do not know what they will tell us and reveal to us in the future. Certainly, though, they will not contradict the Gospels then either, or their origin in heavenly reason. They form a median quantity between heaven and earth. They stand for the reality of redemption, as a seal of the truth of the faith of Christendom. They are two great miracles that tell about the greatest miracle in world history, the Incarnation and Resurrection of the Son of God—as reliable heralds of his coming again in glory.

"If we truly want to know the Face of God, all we have to do is to contemplate the Face of Jesus! In his Face we truly see who God is and what he looks like!"
—Pope Benedict XVI,
September 6, 2006, Rome.

ACKNOWLEDGMENTS

I owe special thanks for the beginning and successful completion of this book to:

Pope Benedict XVI; Bishop Bruno Forte; Msgr. Georg Gänswein; Fr. Carmine Cucinelli, O.F.M. Cap.; Fr. Germano Franco di Pietro, O.F.M. Cap.; Fr. Emilio Cucchiella, O.F.M. Cap.; Fr. Lino Pupatti, O.F.M. Cap.; Fr. Enrico Carusi, O.F.M. Cap.; Fr. Bonaventura Del Romano, O.F.M. Cap.; Fr. Domenico Petracca da Cese, O.F.M. Cap.; St. Pio da Pietrelcina, O.F.M. Cap.; Br. Vincenzo D'Elpidio, O.F.M. Cap.; Sr. Blandina Paschalis Schlömer, O.C.S.O.; Ste. Thérèse de l'enfant Jésus et de la Sainte Face, O. C.D.; Fr. Herbert Douteil, C.S.Sp.; Br. Alan Hall, O.M.V.; Fr. Beda Müller, O.S.B.; Fr. Werner Bulst, S.J.; Fr. Heinrich Pfeiffer, S.J.; Don Giuseppe Ghiberti; Arnold Angenendt; Raam Badde-Morgenthaler; Hans A. Baumann; Benigna Berger; Klaus Berger; Georg and Gisela Bickl; Antonio Bini; Karlheinz Dietz; Walter Dissertori; Mathias Döpfner; Mechthild Flury-Lemberg; Ray Frost; Naidys del Rosario Guerrero Paez; Sandra Hacke; Matthias Henrich; Gaby and Dieter Herbrecht; Michael Hesemann; Markus van den Hövel; Barbara Huth; Niels Christian Hvidt; Dorothea Link; Pia and Antonio de Luca; Bernhard Meuser; Bernhard and Martin Müller; Rudolf Pesch; Josefine Schiffer; Thomas Schmid (who commissioned me to make the last trips of this book for *Die Welt*); Cornelia Schrader; Hildegard Schuhmann; Armin Schwibach; Peter Seewald; Robert Spaemann; Marianne Stutzki; Assunta del Rosso; Ian Wilson—and, naturally, Ellen, dear heart and love of my life.

May God reward them all.

aVe Vera faCIes DoMInI IesV ChrIstI qVI resurreXIt eX InferIs sIs nobIs benIgna hIC et per saeCVLa[1]

pb—Rome, January 6, 2010

CREDITS

Photos:
Paul Badde: End leafs, pp. 2, 4–5, 6–7, 8–9, 10, 20–21, 24, 25, 26, 27, 28–29, 31, 32, 33, 34, 35, 37, 39, 40 above right, 42, 44–45, 46–47, 48, 49, 50, 51, 52–53, 54, 57, 59, 60–61, 63, 64, 66, 67, 68–69, 71, 73, 74–75, 76–77, 78, 80, 82, 83, 84–85, 86, 89, 90, 95, 97, 100, 110–11, 117, 120–21, 124–25, 126–27, 128 above, 129, 130–31, 137, 142–43, 145, 147, 148, 149, 150–51, 152–53, 154, 155, 156, 159.
Hermann Dornhege: p. 40 above right, middle.
Archdiocese of Turin: pp. 13, 14, 16–17, 23.

Matthias Henrich: p. 128 below.
Photo Service—*L'Osservatore Romano*: pp. 18–19, 92–93, 157.
picture-alliance: akg-images: p. 141; dpa, pp. 98–99, 104–5, 106–7, 109, 132–33; dpa-Web p. 103.
Hildegard Schuhmann: pp. 95, 113, 118, 119, 123.
Stadtkirche Bad Wimpfen: p. 114.

Project director: Bernhard Meuser
Graphics editor: Markus Röleke
Book design: Sandra Hacke

[1] "Hail, true face of our Lord Jesus Christ, who rose from the dead; look graciously upon us [lit., may you be gracious to us] now and for eternity." The capitalized letters, if interpreted as Roman numerals, add up to 2009, the year in which the book was written. The dedication on the fast of the Epiphany is the occasion for this word- and number-play (compare the custom of writing the number of the new year in chalk on the lintel over the entrance to the church on that day).—Trans.

VT OES CHRIANI CVI SALVTE DEBENT EIVS ET FORMA QVA INTER HOMINES VERSAP
QVÆ SABAVDORVM METROPOLIS EST PVBLICE VENERADA PROPONITVR ILLVSTR
DECANI SABAVD AVSPICIIS CAROLVS MALLIANVS ARCHID BELLICEN